D0031838

THE MASTER STRATEGIST

Power, Purpose and Principle

THE MASTER STRATEGIST

Power, Purpose and Principle

KETAN J PATEL

HUTCHINSON
LONDON

Published by Hutchinson in 2005

1 3 5 7 9 10 8 6 4 2

Copyright © 2005 by Ketan J. Patel

Hutchinson
The Random House Group Limited
20 Vauxhall Bridge Road, London, SW1V 2SA

Random House Australia (Pty) Limited
20 Alfred Street, Milsons Point, Sydney,
New South Wales 2061, Australia

Random House New Zealand Limited
18 Poland Road, Glenfield
Auckland 10, New Zealand

Random House (Pty) Limited
Endulini, 5a Jubilee Road, Parktown 2193, South Africa

The Random House Group Limited Reg. No. 954009

www.randomhouse.co.uk

A CIP catalogue record for this book
is available from the British Library

Papers used by Random House
are natural, recyclable products made from wood grown in
sustainable forests. The manufacturing processes conform to
the environmental regulations of the country of origin

ISBN 1 8441 3817 8

Typeset by SX Composing DTP, Rayleigh, Essex
Printed and bound in Great Britain by
Mackays of Chatham plc, Chatham, Kent

CONTENTS

In 2001, OECD countries allocated approximately $645 billion[1] to research and development.[2] Three of the largest areas of investment were the fields of medicine, computing and weapons. The success of this investment is clear to all of us in the huge advances that have been made in creating cures for diseases that previously were considered to be incurable, in creating the computational capability to understand things that appeared to be mysteries and in creating bombs that could, if their owners wished, reach across boundaries to destroy whole cities. Whether we translate the fruits of these investments to cure the world, apply computing power to solve the problems that threaten the world or create peace depends on strategy. Strategy, in this context, is simply the name we give to the plans and actions by which we enforce our ways on others – peoples, institutions and environments.

In the field of strategy, we have invested an insignificant fraction of these vast sums. In medical research it is clear that errors can result in death. If we create computing technology that miscalculates we put in jeopardy the systems that this technology runs – everything from aircraft, stock exchanges to heart monitors – and we also risk killing people. If we create inaccurate weapons technology we destroy hospitals instead of arms depots. Yet, we fail to take our research and development of strategic methods with the same seriousness. The strategies we employ have not given us the results we could expect from the breakthroughs we have made. At the end of the 20th century, over 800 million people lived in hunger, 1.1 billion lacked access to safe water and 17 million people died each year from curable diseases. Computing and internet technology was available to only 0.5 to 7 per cent of the populations of Asia, Africa, the Middle East and Africa compared to between 50 and 60 per cent of North Americans. Over 170 million people are estimated to have been killed through war and genocide in the 20th century alone.[3]

Another threat is the pace of the rate of change and the way this is reshaping the world. This more dynamic landscape is the one that strategists need to be able to deal with, yet they are currently equipped and trained to deal with far narrower, more static environments. The best strategic thinking takes a broad view of life and the world, but most comes from sources much earlier than our century, such as Sun Tzu, whose thoughts date from the 5th century BC, Machiavelli, whose book, *The Prince*, was published in the 16th century, Miyamoto Musashi, who wrote in the 17th century and Karl von Clausewitz, who wrote in the 19th century. All of this thinking, however, has its roots in military conflict and so has an in-built bias in that direction.

The breakthroughs in strategic thinking since then have taken a more 'scientific' approach in that they have picked a narrower domain and produced models which address only that particular domain. In addition, because of the lack of investment in developing strategic thought, there have been too few breakthroughs in comparison to other fields, and so we are not well equipped to formulate strategy to deal with the complex series of growing and interconnected factors facing us today.

The progress that has been made in the field of science, for example, has not been matched by that made in the field of strategy, and so we risk squandering the gains made by scientists.

Since the Renaissance, researchers and academic authorities in the fields of science have examined a broad set of narrow domains and established frameworks and formulae that abstract from the complexity to define solutions to very precise problems. The number and diversity of these models of the world provide a rich body of theory and knowledge. In the field of strategy, there has been no such renaissance of thought, and so we do not have the richness or diversity of models to explain the world. However, the models we do have are taken literally and have resulted in narrow and dangerous strategies. These strategies can, and do, lead us to wage unnecessary wars, destroy the environment and over-compete.

To summarise, this work is based on five themes, namely:

1 We are experiencing a level of change that is transforming the context within which strategy needs to be formulated in an exponential and stepped manner.

2 The current methods of developing strategic models will not deliver changes to our strategic methods that are significant or fast enough to deal with the changes in the context.

3 The strategies of today are based on assumptions that are no longer relevant and are based on models that are too simplistic and often erroneous.

4 The level of progress in the fields of science and technology is far ahead of the field of strategy and this is dangerous because strategy is about how we utilise the results of science and technology.

5 The strategists we require cannot be developed quickly enough through the methods we employ today and

development is the responsibility of leaders and individuals and will, in general, require more extreme measures if they wish to succeed.

As a result, in this work, the attempt is to keep the canvas broad. The aim is to consider strategy in the context of a broad and changing world landscape, through the following seven objectives.

- The first objective is to try to make sense of the growing complexity of the world by identifying the most important underlying themes. This is the aim of Chapter one. Given the huge amount of data available to us today, one of the factors to bear in mind is that the value of this data is already in decline and that the value of insight will increase. One set of patterns is drawn out from the mass of change in the world and portrayed as a set of themes or 'shaping phenomena'. It is important to note that whilst these themes may have some value they are by no means complete or lasting.

- The second objective is to identify and explore the problems associated with simplification. This is the aim of Chapter two. It is a critical argument of this work that the current simplification of the world through models is dangerous because it results in simplistic answers to life-threatening problems. And that this simplistic thinking pervades all walks of life from military to personal. Given this argument, this work does not abstract from the data, information and insights used to provide models and frameworks.

- The third objective is to present insights into the nature of strategy and its exercise. This is the aim of Chapter three. To rebalance the bias towards the analytic method, this chapter relies wholly on personal intuition and experience. Its presentation format, but not its content, therefore borrows from the ancient instruction-based tradition.

- The fourth objective is to provide an examination of the exercise of power, purpose and principle. This is the aim of Chapter four. This chapter provides a critique on the existing methods of strategy and provides an alternative based on the insights and arguments of Chapter three.

- The fifth objective is to identify the areas where breakthroughs are required in the field of strategy. This is aim of Chapter five. To be able to add value to the masters of other fields, masters of the field of strategy will need to make leaps that place them ahead of the breakthroughs of other fields. In this chapter we explore the nature of some of these breakthroughs that we need to make in our strategic methods.

- The sixth objective is to lay out an agenda for strategists to address the most fundamental issues and themes of our times. This is the aim of Chapter six. Supercomputers cannot substitute calculation for imagination yet. So they cannot find, imagine or form from obscure bits of data the patterns of possible future scenarios, opportunities or threats. In this chapter we will form such patterns of possibilities as well as lay out a wide-ranging agenda to explore how we can develop greater strategic mastery.

- Finally, we draw together all the strands of thought of this work to summarise the case and agenda for change. This is the aim of the concluding chapter of this work.

This work is aimed at those in all walks of life who have responsibility for developing strategy. Such strategists go by many names. In the White House, they are the policy makers focused on the interests of America – which today know no boundaries and therefore hold the greatest chance to do good as well as the greatest risk of causing disruption and disorder. In the think tanks, they are the political, social and economic analysts who seek to influence the policy makers of the world. On Wall Street, they are the traders, corporate deal advisors and asset managers. In business, they are the executives of major corporations and their advisors. In strategy consulting organisations all around the world, they are analysts aspiring to become what they are already called, strategists. Conventionally, we refer to these people as the strategists and we ignore those that develop strategies in their communities, families and their lives. The scope of this work encompasses the challenges of life and so this conventional definition is challenged. One of the core beliefs underlying this work is that we can only be masters of strategy if we first become masters of ourselves. This is, however, as much a challenge for leaders as it is for individuals.

BEYOND THE CURRENT REALM OF STRATEGY

'Sometimes chaos appears to have order. So, we think we
understand what we observe.'

The Book of Power, Purpose and Principle

Events have crept up on us while we have been immersed
in everyday life. They leave us with problems we cannot solve.
These problems lead us to question every part of our lives.
Regarding politics, how much trust can we put in our leaders?
Can we even be sure they act in our interests? Regarding
society, is our way of life sustainable? Regarding security, are
we safe going about our day-to-day activities? Regarding
economics, do we understand how to sustain our prosperity let
alone expand it to others? Regarding commerce, do we know
how to make money in a world of ever-changing rules?
Regarding the environment, what are the consequences of our
decisions on our world and are we worthy stewards of the
resources of the planet? Regarding technology, is it delivering
benefits or simply disrupting the existing order? On an
individual basis, how well can we look after our loved ones and
can we balance our ambitions, our relationships and our
responsibilities?

Choices seem to lead to more confusion and actions to more
problems. The sheer number of such events that have arisen all
at once leave us unable to rely on the approaches, methods and

formulae of the past. We face the need to rethink our approach. What is the nature of these events and why are they so confusing at this point in history?

Our confusion is due to the many possibilities open to us, which are the result of mankind passing a number of milestones. These milestones have a pattern that we will refer to as The Seven Shaping Phenomena. However, let us not get over-constrained by seven phenomena. This is simply one picture made from the pieces that make up our world.

SEVEN SHAPING PHENOMENA

Phenomenon One: The Breaking of Barriers to Performance

The first phenomenon is the continual and inexorable breaking of barriers, which means performance – particularly human, machine and computing performance – is no longer limited.

THE BREAKING OF HUMAN LIMITATIONS

Men and women are breaking what were previously assumed to be unbreakable barriers both in physical and mental performance. Man has increased his stamina and speed to levels unimaginable a century before. In 2003, the record breaker ran the 26-mile marathon almost 30 per cent faster than his equivalent in the 1897 24.7-mile marathon. Over approximately the same period, Man has jumped nearly 15 per cent further, almost 25 per cent higher and swum the 400 metres freestyle more than 20 per cent faster. During the last 50 years of the 20th century, man even ran the intense 100 metres race almost 10 per cent faster.[1]

Our ability to stretch the human body and mind and challenge the forces of nature has never been so great – and continues to improve. However, this potential has been matched by the abuse of our bodies and minds through means such as drugs, tobacco and food. In 2000, there were 200 million users of illicit drugs. During the 20th century, an estimated 100 million people worldwide died from tobacco-associated diseases. In just over five years up to the year 2000, the number of obese people increased from 200 million to 300 million. The sophistication in production of entertainment drugs continues to grow, with innovations that use new chemicals, including acids. We continue to move towards a world of excessive consumption of anything we desire.[2]

So, at two extremes, we stand on the brink of the Age of Performance *or* the Age of New Decadence.

THE BREAKING OF MACHINE LIMITATIONS

Our inventive creation of machines for almost everything we do has created an era of prosperity never before seen in the history of Man. The pace of machine breakthroughs has grown at an exponential speed. The agricultural era was set to be transformed almost 5,000 years ago with the invention of the basic calculating machine, the abacus. However, breakthroughs in automation and accuracy did not arrive until *c.*200 BC, when the Chinese developed an accurate water clock and an entire automated mechanical orchestra. Even with this platform, it took nearly a thousand years to build the first true mechanical clock in 726 AD. And it was not until 1642, that Pascal invented the first automatic calculating machine for adding and subtracting.

The pace of mechanisation picked up dramatically following the Industrial Revolution in the 18th century, and the world was set to create all manner of production machinery. When he died in 1871, Charles Babbage left behind over 400 square feet of drawings for a computer, his 'Analytic Engine'.[3] The next hundred years saw rapidly accelerating innovations in machine technology being applied to almost every aspect of life. These machines enabled us to further break the barriers of nature, allowing the weakest of men to go faster, further and higher than the previous generation of the highest performing men.

This ability to make almost anything now places us on the edge of truly liberating us from many of the limitations of the human body and many of the barriers of the environment. However, the increasing substitution of machines for men in not only the 'drudgery' of labour but also services, entertainment and other creative endeavours threatens the very role and value of the individual in society.

So, at two extremes, we stand on the brink of the Age of the Rise of Machines *or* the Age of the Fall of Men.

THE BREAKING OF COMPUTING LIMITATIONS

Computing speed doubled every three years in the 40 years to 1950. In the next 20 years it doubled every two years. By 2000, it was doubling every year. In 1997, IBM's Deep Blue Supercomputer defeated the reigning chess champion. In the first few years of the 21st century, a supercomputer being built for the US Department of Energy was expected to have a power of 100 trillion calculations per second – the same processing power, according to the Robotics Institute at Carnegie Mellon University, as the human brain. This is not to suggest that the matching of the human brain by computers is imminent. Based on the number of neurons and connections between neurons, it is estimated that for tasks such as vision, language and motor control, the brain is more powerful than 1,000 supercomputers, but for tasks such as multiplying and searching it is less powerful than a 4-bit microprocessor found in calculators.

The ability to compute the underlying equations of everything – our genetic code, the structure of matter, the nature of time and space – holds out the promise of enabling us to enter a new era of miracles. As early as 1980, American nuclear physicists turned several thousand atoms of lead into gold. In 2000, Chinese scientists cloned six calves from skin cells taken from a bull's ear. In this new era, we will be able to make the crippled walk, the blind see, turn water into wine, feed the multitude and turn base metals into precious ones.[4]

Our capability has never been so great. However, given our emotional failings, particularly our fear of each other and our lust for power, we are prone to turning technological victories into weapons. In the past, this weakness has merely resulted in men destroying men, but in this new era of miracles we have the potential to destroy the genetic essence of man, the fundamental molecular structure of our air, water, rock and life-forms and, once our competence increases, the time-space relationship.

So, at two extremes, we stand on the brink of the Age of Miracles or the Age of the End of Times.

Phenomenon Two: The Unprecedented Mass of Information, Media and Communication

The second phenomenon is the unprecedented mass of information, media and communication available to us across all countries, creeds, socio-economic classes and disciplines.

THE CUMULATIVE HISTORY, KNOWLEDGE AND WISDOM OF MAN AT OUR FINGERTIPS

We now have, through the World Wide Web, unique access to the cumulative information, knowledge and wisdom of

Mankind at our fingertips. This body of information is not, of course, complete, but it is available in enormous quantity and is growing at an exponential rate. It is already accessible to a critical mass of the population of the world and is set to spread all over the world regardless of race, creed, wealth, age or formal education. The estimated time taken for a person to search a random piece of information has been calculated as: nearly 2 months in 1800 working around the clock; just over 5 days by 1900; under a day by 1990; 70 seconds by 2000; and, by 2004, around a second. The search engine of Google has an estimated 4 billion Web pages, which, if printed, would form a stack of paper more than 220 miles high.[5] The ability to free people from the views of their 'master' – parent, teacher, community leader, priest, politician or ruler – has never been so great. Neither has the potential to be confused by the overload, the 'noise'.

So, at two extremes, we stand on the brink of the Age of Freedoms *or* the Age of Confusion.

THE MASS DISSEMINATION OF MEDIA INTO EVERY HOME ON THE PLANET

In the last 25 years of the 20th century, mass-produced media were distributed throughout the world in film from hubs such as Hollywood and Bollywood. The mass media pushed ideas, values and dreams, and pulled demand for the products of its homeland from all over the world. Media are always trying to convince us, the viewer, listener or reader, of something. Their embedded vantage point enables them to do this in many ways. The direct messages we know well – television, radio, newspapers and billboards – because they shout at us from places we expect. The semi-direct messages speak to us from the back of soap packets, on clothing labels, the warning notes in the box of our prescription drug, shop fronts and the many notices and signs that look like information. The indirect messages whisper to us – the newscaster telling us who is a terrorist and who a freedom fighter, the teacher in a classroom telling us the history of the world, the product placed in a our favourite show, the voice we associate with truth and integrity selling us a holiday or insurance. We may not realise we were being sold to, because these messages were embedded in something else, but our subconscious hears the message.

Never before has it been possible to spread propaganda so efficiently. Nor has the potential to be confused by the enormous range of choices ever been so great.

So, at two extremes, we stand on the brink of the Age of Ideas *or* the Age of Propaganda.

MASS PERSON-TO-PERSON-TO-MACHINE COMMUNICATION

The mass availability of communication devices and networks has reached unprecedented levels, enabling the inter-connecting of people to each other, to information and to entertainment. This communication is now possible from home, from work and on the move. In the first few years of the 21st century, 40 per cent of the world had a television, 20 per cent had a personal computer and 17 per cent had a mobile phone. The ability to access people anywhere, any time through any medium was almost a reality. The possibilities for commerce, education and entertainment were enormous. However, the power of the individual to choose continued to rise.

The disruptive next step had already begun: the breaking of the locks that kept intellectual property in the hands of the patent-holder; music and film in the hands of the 'rights' owners, and telecommunications in the hands of the telephone line owners. Open access to intellectual property, entertain-ment and communications for no rent or a rent that is increasingly affordable by a mass global population was nearly a reality. By some estimates, during the early years of the 21st century, 350 million people had used one of the pirate networks to listen to music and more than 2.6 billion copyrighted files had exchanged every month. At the beginning of the 21st century, over 50 per cent of online Americans (38 per cent of all US adults) used their own sources on the internet and considered these to be an important way of finding out what was going on in the world. About 20 per cent of Americans considered the internet a top source for election news and used it to supplement or supercede broadcasting or paper-based news media, newspapers and magazines.[6]

People's ability to create their own networks, build their own content libraries and educate themselves has never been so substantial. Nor has the ability of the official channels and suppliers to lose the 'loyalty' of customers ever been so pronounced.

So, at two extremes, we stand on the brink of the Age of the Networked Society *or* the Age of Individualism.

Phenomenon Three: The Compression of Time, Distance and Access

The third phenomenon is the compression or collapse of time, price, distance and access. This has resulted in a greater ability to reach wider audiences, and a new ability to participate at unprecedented speed.

THE DESTRUCTION OF TIME LIFE CYCLES, COLLAPSE OF PRICE AND THE RISE IN AFFORDABILITY

We are seeing the collapse of time. This is evident in the collapse in the life cycles of our products and services. By the end of the 20th century, the time it took to launch a product, the time before returns could be harvested, the time before the product became irrelevant and the time necessary to launch the replacement had collapsed across a wide range of industries from shoes to electronics to entertainment media. The service industries, such as management consulting, IT services and business process outsourcing, remained as 'higher value' realms. However, within the first few years of the 21st century, the time value of these had also collapsed due to over-supply, destructive price competition and the participation of lower cost countries such as India and China. The reduction in prices of products and services led to an increase in the affordability of all things consumer. From almost zero usage at the end of the Second World War, television, telephone, mobile phones and household appliances were, by the turn of the 20th century, within the grasp of the mass population of the world.

Our ability to move faster through the process of invention-destruction-replacement has never been so accentuated. However, we are also entering an era of ever-increasing quality coupled with ever-decreasing prices. As a result, our uncertainty as to how to create a sustainable system of enterprise has never been so much under strain.

So, at two extremes, we stand on the brink of the Age of Compression of Time and Space *or* the Age of Compression of Value.

THE COLLAPSE OF DISTANCE

Geographical barriers have been destroyed by the rise of international travel. The Superpowers in history have always attracted merchants, artists and migrant workers. America, like Alexandria, Rome and London before her, has been a magnet for adventurers, pioneers and power, fame and wealth seekers. The time it takes to travel from England to New York has shrunk from 18 days in the 1830s, using steam power, to 6½ hours by aeroplane. In the first few years of the 21st century, about 540 million people per year travelled to places that in previous eras were considered to be the privilege of the wealthy. They stayed on average only a week.[7]

Our ability to reach every part of the globe quickly and easily for trade and leisure has never been so great. Nor has our ability to move around the world swiftly and with secrecy in order to engage in war, terrorism and environmental disruption ever been so great.

So, we stand on the brink of the Age of Global Reach *or* the Age of Global Disruption.

THE DENSITY OF POPULATION

Population densities have risen dramatically throughout history. The largest city in 3100 BC was believed to be Memphis, Egypt, with a population of 30,000. In 612 BC, Babylon was the first to pass 200,000. In 637 AD, Baghdad, Iraq, was the first city to have over 1 million inhabitants. In 1825, the record was held by London, which had a population of 5 million. By 1925, the record had passed to New York, which had a population of 10 million and by 1965, this record was broken by Tokyo, which had 20 million inhabitants.[8]

In 1800, only 3 per cent of the world's population lived in urban areas. By 1900, this had risen to 14 per cent. By 1950, this had risen to 30 per cent and by 2000, 47 per cent of the world's population lived in urban centres. Wealth density had also risen sharply, to the extent that by the end of the 20th century, the top 20 countries had over 50 times the wealth of the bottom 20.[9]

In the early 21st century, this population pattern was set to continue. The appetite of the dense and wealthy cities to consume labour could not be matched by their own indigenous populations. The expectation for the first wave of modernised countries of the 20th century, countries such as Japan, Germany, France, the UK and America, was that they would need millions of migrants in order for their cities to function. In the meantime, at the dawn of the 21st century, the high potential economies, particularly China and India, began to feel the wealth of the first wave countries pass into their hands. With it, millions thronged to their major cities. China declared the creation of 50 silicon valleys, of which a dozen appeared to be the most promising, and government funding of between $50 to $70 billion for innovation. This, coupled with the $60 billion or so of annual foreign direct investment in its lands, meant that these valleys became magnets for talented people.[10]

Our ability to create wealth continues to be concentrated in more and more centres and has never been so pronounced. Nor has our ability to threaten the wealth creation of existing centres ever been so great. With the emergence of the new valleys, the threat to the American Silicon Valley, the Japanese consumer electronics hubs, the South Korean broadband economic centres, the Singaporean Financial hub and the technology and bio-technology European hubs in the UK, Germany, France and Ireland has also never been so great.

So, at two extremes, we stand on the brink of the Age of Silicon Valleys *or* the Age of the Destructive Competition of Valleys.

Phenomenon Four: The Unlocking of Creativity from Every Corner of the World

The fourth phenomenon is the unlocking of creativity from every corner of the world based on more invention, more knowledge workers and more participation.

THE EXPONENTIAL RISE IN INVENTION

In 1843, the head of the US patent organisation was famously quoted as saying that we were nearing the point at which human advancement must end. Although it is unclear whether he actually believed this point to be imminent, no one could have predicted the unlocking of the inventive potential of Man that began in the 20th century.

The combination of war and ideology, Capitalism vs. Communism, drove Man to break new barriers. A series of races began. The race to process political intelligence drove the building of supercomputers. The race to possess the biggest threat drove the creation of atomic weapons. The race to power the factories drove the building of nuclear power plants. The race to declare the superiority of one way over another, drove the landing of men on the moon. At the end of this period, we had super-computing, super-weapons, super-energy and super-terrestial space vehicles. America, as the leading culture of technology and enterprise, drove the revolutions in internet access and media distribution. This culminated in the internet boom in the year 2000. And so, we entered the 21st century with the core technologies that would enable us to make the next breakthroughs. These core technologies enabled us to begin to break the quantum code of atoms, the nano code of matter and the gene code of man.

Never before have we ridden the momentum of so much inventive potential. Nor have the ethical-moral-spiritual codes by which we live ever felt so inadequate to deal with the potential dangers that face us as a result of our inventions.

So, at two extremes, we stand on the brink of the Age of Super-Science *or* the Age of the Science of Mass Destruction.

THE 'MACHINE-LIKE' PRODUCTION OF TECHNOLOGY, DESIGN AND ENGINEERING RESOURCES

To fuel this creativity, we needed to be able to manufacture machines and skilled resources. The new era was to be led by people labelled 'Knowledge Workers'. Their role was the transformation of materials through expert knowledge. This use of knowledge promised to lead us to new prosperity.

During the 20th century, the rise of America, and its trade with its allies, had resulted in the biggest bank of knowledge assets – people and intellectual property rights – being held on its shores. Their example led the Japanese to participate more effectively in the global business world during the 1980s. In the last two decades of the 20th century, the Chinese, and then the Indians, also began to participate more effectively. Although it is difficult to be precise, it is estimated that, in 2000, approximately 200,000 engineers graduated from Chinese universities and technical colleges. A similar number also passed through India's colleges. Within a few years this had risen to between 300,000 and 400,000 for both China and India, with each country producing nearly three times the number of engineers produced in America. By various estimates, the wage cost of their engineers was between a quarter and a tenth of the equivalent American engineer. Many European countries closed their science departments and fell a long way behind in the race to produce engineering talent. In the early 21st century, the Americans began to lose confidence that they could compete against the volume and cost of these Asian engineers. The participation of China and India began to be seen as a threat to American prosperity. Some Americans seemed to forget that not only did they have a huge lead, but also the most talented and advanced bank of intellectual property in the world.[11]

We have never been able to produce such large volumes of

knowledgeable human talent. We have also never had such a powerful ability to deploy this talent in trade and commercial battles.

So, at two extremes, we stand on the brink of the Age of Knowledge Workers *or* the Age of the Battle of Knowledge Economies.

THE RISE IN KNOWLEDGE AND PARTICIPATION OF POORER NATIONS

After the Second World War, the emphasis shifted from military warfare to propaganda and corporate warfare. Soviet Russia and America built up corporations, universities, armies and intelligence agencies, and competed to win minds, create power and build wealth. By the end of the 20th century, America had won a victory that seemed so complete and undisputed that the American Way stood poised to sweep the world. Popular media coverage defined this system as the ideology of capitalism: democracy, free trade and globalisation. The world, particularly the Chinese and Indians, seemed to accept the core aspects of the system and the ideology. Slowly, almost imperceptibly at first, the Chinese and Indians built their resources. By 2004, the notion of the rise of the BRIC countries (Brazil, Russia, India and China), especially the rise and rise of China and India, had gained popular recognition. Unfortunately, it was a time of global uncertainty and insecurity, and the reaction of the ideological victors of the 20th century to the successful participation of the Chinese and Indians was to protect their status. This was despite the fact that, in that period, the combined revenue of the top six corporations, all from the existing wealthy nations, exceeded the national budgets of 30 nations representing 50 per cent of the world's population.

Our ability to break new scientific barriers, to invent and to produce has never been so great. In the early 21st century, the growing appetite of the consuming billions of China and India even offered the potential to involve Africa in a prosperity revolution. Unfortunately, our inclination to deploy our knowledge workers in international and intra-national commercial battles seems greater. The message to the poorer nations is that the ideology is hollow: self-interest will, as often happens in history, drive policy.

So, at two extremes, we stand on the brink of the Age of Global Prosperity *or* the Age of Self-Interest and Protectionism.

Phenomenon Five: The Connectivity of People through Multiple Global Systems

The fifth phenomenon is the connectivity of the world's people through multiple global systems: information and communication systems, personal payment systems and capital market systems.

INTERCONNECTION THROUGH THE WORLD WIDE WEB, GLOBAL MEDIA AND GLOBAL TELECOMS CHANNELS

The Persians gave Alexander the Great a communication system that linked his entire empire. The Roman Empire used a system that linked every soldier to his beloved in Rome. The British Empire used the railway network to connect the cities within every nation they conquered, thus allowing the free flow of trade and communication, and the control of the indigenous people. It would take the information technology revolution to make the most fundamental changes in how we connect with each other. During the technology boom of the final years of the 20th century, a number of technologies arose that connected Man to machines and people to each other. These technologies were computing, land telecommunications, land and satellite media networks, mobile communications and all manner of sensors. At the beginning of the 21st century, the networks and devices of each of these largely separate technologies began to converge and become interoperable. They were ready to be unified by a World Wide Web.

Never before have we had the ability to connect everyone and everything to everyone and to everything else. Not only are the rich, privileged and free connected, but the most poor, most under-privileged and most abused people are on the verge of having access to the ideas and people that could be their saviours. The early 21st century use of the internet, however, shows that the overwhelming propensity is to use this grand capability for pornography, gambling and gossip. Hence the possibility of using this technology primarily for propaganda and trivia is great.

So, at two extremes, we stand on the brink of the Age of Communication *or* the Age of Trivial Pursuits.

CONNECTION TO FINANCIAL RESOURCES AND FREEDOM TO SPEND THROUGH GLOBAL PAYMENT SYSTEMS

In almost all our history, people have been divided into those that have the cash to pay and those that do not. This separation will remain at some level. However, for a huge number of people, and for the majority of their purchases, whether for a bar of chocolate or a car, this divide has been broken.

At the start of the 21st century, the global payment card was one of the symbols of consumer capitalism, freeing people from being constrained by their immediate ability to afford what they desired. It also allowed them to access their money all over the world and to pay without carrying cash. This was achieved from villages in Myanmar to the streets of Manhattan. The global payment system of Visa International enabled people to spend beyond their means. Around a trillion dollars worth of American and British credit card transactions went through the payment systems of the world. In the first few years of the 21st century, it was already clear that the Asians would follow this pattern of behaviour.

The ability of people all over the world to pay for their aspirations and dreams has never been so great. Nor has the ability for payment system providers to exploit our desire to live fantasies that we cannot afford ever been so exaggerated.

So, at two extremes, we stand on the brink of the Age of Personal Financial Freedom *or* the Age of Personal Financial Greed.

CONNECTIVITY OF CAPITAL MARKETS AND THEIR ABILITY TO SHIFT MONEY THROUGH GLOBAL FINANCIAL TRADING SYSTEMS

Through the ages, the trade of the world has flowed through physical centres where traders met to place their bets and reap the rewards. The ancient historic centres included Athens, Alexandria, Rome and Constantinople. At the end of the influence of these great centres, there was a period of relative stagnation in Europe. Between the 11th century and the 18th century, the growth in material wealth across Europe and North America was negligible. By the 19th century, the growth was almost 200 per cent and in the 20th century almost 2000 per cent. By the end of the 20th century, Man had experienced the greatest wealth creation in history, and New York and London had become the dominant centres.[12]

In the late 20th century, technology, knowledge and access enabled capital to flow more freely than ever before to markets all over the world. In the last 25 years of the century, the stock markets of Asia (although still comparatively small) outstripped the American and British markets in growing their value. Asian markets grew 80 per cent in the technology sector compared to the American and British markets' 14 per cent, in retail 23 per cent to their 14 per cent and in financial services 20 per cent to their 16 per cent. In fact, in all industries other than pharmaceuticals the Asian markets outperformed the American and British capital markets and, in all but telecoms, outperformed the Japanese. This is not to say that the Asians were the greatest beneficiaries.[13]

The free flow of capital and access to international trading centres enabled the smartest capitalists to make money. These pioneers were mostly American and took the form of large scale institutional investors, specialist trading entities labelled 'hedge funds', private equity and venture capitalists and private individuals. This money differed enormously in how far ahead it looked and how long it held its investments. The money that made the greatest returns was often the fastest in and out of investments and the most speculative. Its largest impact was during the Asian crisis, when nearly 75 per cent was knocked off the capital market value of Indonesia and South Korea. Thailand and the Philippines dropped by between 30 and 40 per cent. A new type of raider was born. Perversely, these were the most 'open' of Asian markets in terms of their accessibility to foreign investors. This openness was considered to be a key factor in the development of these countries. On the other hand, China and India, who had not participated in the liberalisation of their capital markets, saw their value fall only 1 per cent and 10 per cent respectively.[14]

The ability of the smartest capitalists to invest all over the world has never been greater. This means that, more than ever before, innovators worldwide have a unique ability to access funding for their ideas. However, given the short-term nature of the flow of money, particularly some of the most profitable money, the ability to shake the financial stability of nations has also never been greater.

So, at two extremes, we stand on the brink of the Age of Capitalism *or* the Age of Capitalists.

Phenomenon Six: The Rise of Fixed Positions and Asymmetry

The sixth phenomenon is the rise of fixed positions and asymmetry fuelled by the rise of ideology, unequal war and the structural differences between nations.

THE TRANSFORMATION OF RELIGION AND THE RISE OF IDEOLOGY

Looking through the long sweep of history, we see the rise and fall of religions. Through the rise of Greece and Rome, their gods remained a national construct, but both Superpowers were inclusive of the gods of others. Indeed, it is said that, on his journeys, Alexander the Great embraced the ways of the Persians and took with him the spiritualists of India. With the rise of Christianity, we see the rise of the largest and most global religion. Christianity, in its many different forms, was spread with zeal by the European empires to Africa, the Middle East and Asia through ideological and mercantile crusades. Judaism also became a global force in every major capital, although its people spread without any ideological aspirations to convert the local populace. Hinduism spread throughout the Indian subcontinent. Buddhism spread to China, South East Asia and Japan. The newer religion of Islam became a regional force in the Middle East and in South East Asia.

As Man questioned the teachings of the Church during the 15th-century Renaissance of the arts and sciences, Christianity gradually became less of an ideological force and more of a cultural norm. Slowly, church-goers declined and, in many parts of the world, this cultural norm evaporated too. At the end of the Second World War, people in many parts of the world felt a renewed liberation. Although religions had become global, the ideological force that had spread them and instilled them into people's lives in the main no longer existed. By the end of the 20th century, the internet provided the possibility for almost all the world, regardless of creed, to examine the word of Christ and embrace the instruction to love their neighbour as well as the word of the Buddha and seek enlightenment. Christianity in the West had become more of a social affair and Hinduism and Buddhism more of a personal spiritual affair. Judaism remained a personal and community matter for a very successful global diaspora of Israelites. Only Islam remained a strong ideological force. In reaction to what was often referred to as a 'fundamentalist' Islam, new and more strident strains of Christianity, Judaism and Hinduism emerged. The leaders of peoples from countries where these more strident strains were taking root were able to present arguments through the global media networks that advocated war, assassination, segregation and brutal retaliation in ways that convinced mass populations whilst claiming to follow the teachings of their religions.

The ability of the world to reach and embrace the spiritual instruction of the great religious leaders of history has never been so great. However, in the face of their enemy, the ability to re-invigorate ideology remains just as strong.

So, at two extremes, we stand on the brink of the Age of Higher Consciousness *or* the Age of the Battle of Ideologies.

ASYMMETRIC WARS AND BATTLES, AND THE RISE OF SMALL FORCES

Large forces fighting small ones is not a new concept to the world. Every major superpower has forced itself on smaller nations to seize land, people and other resources. At their peak empires have taken huge amounts of land. The Byzantine Empire covered just over 2 million square miles in 550 AD, the Arab Empire around 11 million square miles in 700, the Mongol Empire around 25 million square miles in 1300, the Ming Empire around 7.5 million square miles in 1450, the Ottoman Empire around 5 million square miles from 1600 to

1900 and, in the 20th century, the British Empire covered nearly 35 million square miles.[15]

At the start of the 21st century, America has one of the biggest homelands of any Superpower in history and an unprecedented level of influence through trade, foreign direct investment, media distribution, global corporations, capital markets participation and the sale of American products and services. After one of the great unpredicted events of history, the attack on the Twin Towers in New York on 11 September 2001, America decided it was time to assert its enormous military might on the small but determined forces of its enemies. The American military and defence budget for 2003 was over $400 billion. This made America the first potential Hyperpower in history. However, America also possessed 2,450 landmark buildings, 2,800 power stations and 55,000 community water systems; it had 12 million cargo containers entering the country, 500 million foreign visitors and 95,000 miles of border, plus financial transactions worth $11 trillion were processed through the New York Stock Exchange to support its economic power. Can such a large country protect itself from a small, determined and covert force?[16]

The ability of a Superpower to wage war has never been so great. Nor has the potential for a Superpower to lose as much against a small force been so great.

So, at two extremes, we stand on the brink of the Age of Hyperpower or the Age of the End of Superpower.

STRUCTURAL DIFFERENCES BETWEEN NATIONS

The 20th century produced new labels for the prosperous and the poor. The former were called the Developed World and the latter the Developing or Third World. This language was also used in an absolute sense by members of the 'Developed World', who thereby implicitly assumed that history had come to an end and that the score could now be taken. They reached the conclusion that the Developed World had won. Only to find, a few years later, in the first few years of the 21st century, it was clear that this language was inadequate and the conclusion premature. The labels needed to be far more sophisticated if they were to recognise the progress of China, India and other countries in South East Asia, as well as some of the countries of Latin America, Eastern Europe and the Middle East. Even amongst the largely lagging African countries there were differences worthy of note, such as Botswana. In addition, smaller regions and cities such as Hong Kong and Singapore and the countries of Scandinavia led a healthier, more prosperous, more caring and less corrupt way of life than the rest of the Developed World. The need for a new analysis and new language was evident but did not yet exist.

The most disadvantaged countries consisted of those with the worst structural conditions: harsh weather plagued them with drought, despotic rulers with communal violence and harsh living conditions, combined with a lack of effective institutions of education and employment. In 2003, this structural poverty led to 1.1 billion people, roughly one-sixth of the world's population, not having access to safe water. In addition 2.6 billion people, roughly two-fifths of the world's population, lacked access to adequate sanitation. By contrast, 80 per cent of global resources were used by the world's richest countries, who represent only 20 per cent of the global population. This inequality was reinforced by the fact that the wealth of the world's 11 richest people was equivalent to that of the 49 least developed countries, standing at £136.5bn.[17]

Our ability to address structural poverty has never been so pronounced given the financial, intellectual and commercial resources we possess. Nor has our ability to continue to ignore the world just around the corner been so heightened.

So, at two extremes, we stand on the brink of the Age of Plenty *or* the Age of Structural (In)Differences.

Phenomenon Seven: The Presence of Overwhelming Latent Power

The seventh phenomenon is the existence of overwhelming power to destroy, win wars and justify our means and our ends.

THE ABILITY TO DESTROY THE WORLD MANY TIMES OVER

Great invention has led to great weaponry, and the quest for great weaponry has led to great invention. The early waves of invention – the wheel, gunpowder, steel – all provided weapons for personal combat or battlefield combat. Subsequent inventions – aircraft, computing, atomic reactions – armed us with weapons of mass destruction. In the Superpower race of the 20th century between the Soviet Union and America, the weapons of mass destruction were stock-piled. After the collapse and dissolution of the USSR, these weapons, and the experts that understood the underlying technology, spread to a wider set of countries.

The Iraq War of 2003 was a critical milestone for a number of reasons. It had the potential to reshape relationships in the Middle East, to regulate one of the biggest oil reserves in the world, to dismantle a regime widely accepted as pernicious, to send a warning to enemy states of the US on the consequences of their enmity and to enhance the Iraqi people's ability to embrace democracy. However, the outcome showed failings in political assessment, strategy and tactics, and was, initially, far from realising the positive outcome some had hoped for. The lessons learnt by the enemies of America were: possess and be prepared to use nuclear weapons; in the absence of nuclear weapons, lose the battle quickly and then wage a long and patient guerrilla war; sabotage the political aims of America, for example, by dividing them from their allies; linking with neighbouring countries to influence the politics of the conquered land; and, most of all, by being patient. The gap between intention and outcome can lead to onerous unintended consequences. With the increased destructive potential of our weapons the negative consequences are set to be more severe.

Our ability to destroy has never been so extreme. Our ability to restrict our destructive capacity seems to be slipping from our hands.

So, at two extremes, we stand on the brink of the Age of Strategic Military Intervention *or* the Age of Political Misadventure.

THE ABILITY TO WIN WARS FASTER THAN EVER BEFORE

The empires of history have been built on the might and effectiveness of their military. Speed and flexibility was primarily applied to battle tactics and personal combat and not to whole wars. By the early 21st century, the potential to change the nature of war itself was in our grasp. The ability to annihilate the enemy from afar had continued to grow. The musket against the sword became the aerial bombing campaign against the entrenched enemy. We could now flatten the enemy's positions, part of the enemy's land or, if we wished, all of the enemy's land and then proceed to negotiate with the ruined.

The First and Second World Wars in the first half of the 20th century lasted 4 and 7 years respectively, and resulted in an estimated total of 37 million casualties in the First World War an estimated total of 61 million casualties in the Second. In the last decade of the 20th century, the first Iraq War took approximately 6 weeks to conclude. The second Iraq War of

2003 lasted approximately half that time. Superpowers could conclude the 'formal' armed struggle part of their wars faster than ever before.

However, the American soldier, who was briefed to believe that he was a liberator of the Iraqi people, was instead more often stoned, spat on, cursed and shot at. Fast wars did not exhaust and defeat the mind of the enemy, who was willing to fight on after the aggressors had declared victory. Unlike the aftermath of the long wars of previous periods in history when the victors could enforce their rule, in later wars conquered lands could not easily be transformed and reconstructed.

Similarly, we were better able to win wars between corporations faster than ever before. The rise of the large-scale merger and acquisition had created enterprises with enormous scale at a global level. In the year 2000 alone, 39,499 deals, valued at $3.4 trillion, were done between companies buying or merging with other companies.[18]

Our ability to win wars has never been so clear. However, our ability to win peace is a substantial challenge.

So, at two extremes, we stand on the brink of the Age of Fast Wars *or* the Age of Continuous War because we are unable to win peace.

THE ABILITY TO PROPAGATE IDEOLOGY AS A CONSTANT STREAM TO MASS POPULATIONS

There are forces within the seven phenomena described above which underscore the ability to influence mass populations. These forces are: the history, knowledge and wisdom of Man at our fingertips; the mass push of media into every home on the planet; mass person-to-person-to-machine communication; interconnection through the World Wide Web, global media channels and global telecoms; and the collapse of religion allied to the rise of ideology.

These forces present each individual with the greatest potential for becoming materially and spiritually free. These forces also present each power-wielder with enormous potential for indoctrinating people. The potential exists for someone to create a message that combines political and religious ideology, entertainment and the promise of material success.

So, never before have individuals had the ability to have access to so much information, develop their own information networks and learn so much. Equally, never before has the power of ideology been so well backed by media impact and reach. As a result, never before have we had the power to reshape assumptions, beliefs and aspirations so effectively.

So, at two extremes, we stand on the brink of the Age of Individual Freedom *or* the Age of Ideological Enslavement.

PHENOMENAL COMPLEXITY AND THE FUNDAMENTAL QUESTIONS FOR LEADERS

The world situation, described through the Seven Shaping Phenomena above, is both ripe with opportunity and fraught with danger. The resulting challenges are beyond the scope of current leaders and current strategic methods. What we are experiencing is profound because it represents the biggest challenge yet to our thinking. The challenges to leaders of companies, societies and governments are overwhelming because these challenges threaten our ability to create peace, prosperity and freedom. These are the Great Challenges of our times.

The Great Challenges

1   How to deal with the inexorable rise in expectations as barriers are broken.
2   How to find meaning from the confusing and overwhelming volume of information and dis-information.
3   How to survive in a world of ever-rising volume and ever-decreasing prices and an ever-increasing reliance on machines for satisfaction.
4   How to maintain the value of our assets as others instantly copy and exceed us.
5   How to make sense of a world in which people, information and money move freely around the globe.
6   How to avoid ignoring those who live with poverty, brutality and oppression as victims and perpetrators.
7   How to fight those who appear undeterrable in their opposition to our way of life.
8   How to deal with an unlimited capacity to destroy.
9   How to unlock the potential of people.

One way of understanding the events that challenge us is to use the Seven Phenomena. However, we must not see each phenomenon as a stand-alone force or become attached ourselves to these seven. Each phenomenon multiplies as it interacts with other phenomena to create events that are beyond our current approaches. This is the greatest challenge facing Man. The nature of this challenge is common to governments, organisations and individuals.

Fundamental Causes

There are five fundamental causes of the problems we face.

1 Inappropriate Physical Strategies: We try to impose outcomes on situations. As the variables (like the variables in a mathematical equation) defining a situation have moved beyond our experience, our ability to create coherent strategies has become compromised. Our views of situations have become inadequate. For example, previously we could depend on an understanding of what a large force could do to a small one but a number of factors, in particular technology and information, have altered this.

The breaking of physical norms is happening at a pace that outstrips the old strategic formulae.

2 Inappropriate Emotional Strategies: This prediction of behaviour has been shaken by a number of key forces. Firstly, the world has become 'smaller' in terms of our ability to reach it. Secondly, we have become used to quick results, partly because of the increasing power of money to deliver results. Thirdly, we cannot act in a way that is invisible to our public. The result is that as the strong have imposed themselves on an increasing number of the weak more quickly than ever before they have created potential responses that are unpredictable. The consequence of previous strategies is populations infused with fear, anger and hatred. Given the growing ability of these populations to access technology and capital, and to travel, the ability to predict their response is waning.

The old formula for predicting the behaviour of populations is inadequate.

3 Inappropriate Competitive Strategies: We adopt a win–lose approach. The legacy of simplistic conquest-based strategy has permeated all walks of life. Governments, businesses and individuals all compete to accrue power and wealth. Information has enabled us to draw up league tables for almost all activities and to publish the results, from education to business. The biggest are judged to be the winners and, as a result, we sacrifice many other values. However, the sustainability of success judged in this way has been shaken by fundamental changes in technology; shortening of the time needed to deliver products; our global access to markets; the ability to allow capital to flow freely to the best ideas; and the free flow of information. Some have moved against this more competitive mode and sought to forge a middle path through 'soft alliances', so called because they are not based on the exchange of ownership stakes. The inadequacy of such strategies in delivering successful results has also been exposed.

The dissolving of barriers to competition has resulted in old strategic formulae becoming inadequate.

4 Inappropriate Monetary Strategies: We focus on money, in particular, over other objectives. In addition, the desired results of ambitious people often split into power and fame. A number of critical factors enable their pursuit. The first is the ability to specialise in all walks of life, which creates opportunities for more and more diversity so that more of us can succeed without fighting each other. The second is the growth of capital, which enables us to fund almost any venture in any part of the world. The third is the rise in the capacity to invent new products, which gives us the ability to translate our dreams into realities faster than ever before. This results in an unprecedented number of choices. However, choice is primarily controlled by one factor: the control mechanism for all of these things is the return on investment. Since the capital markets allocate capital based on the return on investment and it increasingly wants these returns faster, many agendas will remain unsatisfied. So the way these capital markets are run has the most significant impact on what is achieved. With the purpose of making money at the heart of our strategies, we increasingly address a smaller proportion of the issues and the things that add value to people's lives.

The over-focus of resources on the acquisition of wealth leads to a loss of emphasis on other issues and to the exclusion of those who cannot play by the rules of capital. These factors have revealed the inadequacy of today's strategic formulae.

5 *Inappropriate Spiritual Strategies:* We fail to build awareness, control and purpose. For the sake of simplicity, let us take spiritual to mean something beyond the 'surface' of everyday life, such as physical possessions and sensory entertainments, something that touches an innate sense of fulfilment in people.

Three forces in particular are counteracting the pursuit of a more virtual path. Firstly, the increasing volume and effectiveness of mass media desensitises us and threatens to overwhelm our judgement. Secondly, the number of events outside of our control that have the potential to significantly change our lives continues to rise. Thirdly, the global rise of a capital culture leads to the mass desire and pursuit of personal wealth. So we act with the hope that the acquisition of this wealth provides us with the huge potential to change things for the better. However, the desire for personal wealth overwhelms us and, since we cannot all succeed, the majority are dissatisfied.

The old formulae of religions for increasing awareness, providing people with more control over their lives and enabling them to pursue a higher purpose are inadequate in helping us to overcome these counteracting forces.

An increasing number of variables are present in every situation facing leaders. These variables appear to be increasing in potency due to the recent advances in the performance of people and machines. As a result, things that we thought were simple, and therefore predictable, seem to be far more complex. Our understanding of these complex factors only increases our uncertainty. The fundamental truths that we relied on previously seem less fundamental. However, the sources of this uncertainty are fundamental; they are physical, emotional, monetary, competitive and spiritual changes.

In the next chapter, we will examine the adequacy of our existing strategic methods, and the impact these methods have on the strategy of a number of entities, in particular governments, investors and corporations, as well as on individuals.

THE LOSS OF RELEVANCE

'Strategies are destroyed when they become fads. Plagiarism destroys strategies and absolute plagiarism destroys strategies absolutely.'

The Book of Power, Purpose and Principle

BEHAVIOUR AS CONTEXT FOR STRATEGY

One reading of history is to see it as the story of Man's search for meaning. History shows us that this search begins in every culture once the basic need for survival and security has been addressed. The search has taken many paths. The paths include the hunter, the feudal–imperial, personal spiritual, religious, industrial and technological, idealist and capitalist.

Each path gives us insights into Man's pattern of behaviour. Between 10,000 and 1000 BC, strong forces of feudal conquest led to the move from the path of the hunter to mass civilisations all over the world. Civilisations were established through the feudal–imperial path. The early Chinese, Egyptian, Indian, Greek and Roman empires all flourished during these periods, and emperors replaced kings, who had replaced chiefs. These empires became corrupted over time and lost their superior edge. All over the world, for the next thousand years, great spiritual leaders showed people a new spiritual path to enlightenment. Moses, Zoroaster, the Buddha and Christ and philosophers such as Confucius and Plato showed one way. Their intensely personal insights were taken over by the leaders who, for the next 1,500 years or so, established the path of religion by organising followers of the faiths. Christianity, Islam, Buddhism and Hinduism established their roots all over the world. From the 16th to the 18th century, much of the world questioned the teachings of the organised religions and forged a path of exploration, industrialisation and scientific enquiry. Chinese technology led the world until the 18th century, when European progress took over. The economic powers warred and conquered and established their hold on blocks of the world. They were ready for the great 20th century wars of ideals. Fascism, Communism and Capitalism fought and, by the end of the 20th-century, the path of Capitalism had won. In its victory lie the seeds of its downfall.

At each stage, the advocates of the prevailing path have declared victory over the previous one. In each successive path, the previous path retains some hold but, because of the nature of our victory mentality, the prevailing path undermines the previous one. Only by destroying do we seem to find the power that we seek. We find ourselves today more prosperous than ever before, but with more power to create or destroy than ever before. With all this power, we have circled back to the need for survival and security. The quality of our strategies will determine the outcome from here on.

Each path has had its strategists. The cumulative experience of Man's strategic thought has not been available to us until the last decade of the 20th century. The internet, the spread of personal computers, broadband networks and the collapsing price of the printed word have led to the exponential growth of the collection and dissemination of thought throughout the world. In every era before us, strategists have had to find the answers almost afresh, and with much less access to wisdom from previous eras. Given the unprecedented resources available to us today, how appropriate are our strategies and strategists for addressing the multiplicity of challenges we face today?

The unfortunate answer is that we have been conned. At best we have erred. We have erred on the most fundamental things. Erred in believing that the analysis will reveal the answer. Erred in believing that we are strategists. Erred in believing that analytic frameworks, methods, models and formulae would make us strategists.

There are two basic reasons for our errors. The first has its source in the political and social democratisation process. This has led us to believe that democracy requires equality far beyond basic and fundamental liberties. This belief has pervaded democratic societies at all levels, particularly in our education systems and amongst employers and governments, where it has been enthusiastically adopted, with the result that labels are applied that are factually incorrect. The equality of labels leads us to call a draughsman an architect, an illustrator a designer and an analyst a strategist. Analysts, as an essential ingredient in the process of strategy formulation, examine data and structure it for further examination. Using frameworks, the analyst may also provide possible actions. However, given the rigid and deterministic nature of frameworks, the possible actions will be formulaic. It requires a strategist to see the possibilities for action, for winning and losing.

The second basic error comes from a rigid adherence to the rational approach. The problem is one of 'recency', that is, too much credibility is given to the recent past. Man's recent past and most profound physical breakthroughs have been driven by the rational scientific path. These breakthroughs are wide ranging and include industrial, medical, computing, agricultural and transportation technologies. As a result, the most influential people in society are the 'rational' intellectual elite – as opposed to an intuitive, religious or spiritual one. Their approach assumes that the answer to all things can be reached through an analytic method and can be processed by Man to arrive at complete solutions. The danger lies not in analysis, but in the assumption of its completeness as an approach. The danger lies not in processing, but in the assumption of its absoluteness. These problems are compounded by the victory mentality that denies alternative approaches. A subsidiary problem is that today's winners are Western logicians and strategists, who assume that the Greeks were the inventors of formalised logic, and the Europeans the inheritors. This poorly founded assumption ignores two of the other early rich streams of thought regarding logic and the scientific method: the exploration of logic and reason in the 5th century BC by the Indian philosopher Dignaga, and the Ancient Indian logic and case-based reasoning of the 1st and 2nd centuries AD, and the Chinese Taoist use of the scientific method around 5th century BC, when the philosopher Lao-tzu, like the Greeks and Indians, explored the nature of reality and knowledge. The victory mentality has led to a lack of adequate exploration of the fruits of other cultures and their streams of thought.

Our greatest educational institutions teach analysis and call it strategy. Our greatest corporations employ analysts and call them strategists. Our greatest advisory institutions provide their clients with analysts and call them strategists. We could argue that these are merely labels. We could argue that the truth is already recognised: the youngster named a strategist is merely an apprentice under a much older head who is the real strategist. In fact, most often the much older head is just a more aged analyst. The language is important. The false labels have eroded our integrity. We have stopped being discerning.

THE FAILURE OF MODERN STRATEGY

<u>Strategy is fundamentally about difference</u>. Strategy therefore denies equality, striving for sameness or belief in there being only one answer. Difference requires leaps beyond what others can grasp. Strategy requires us to go beyond:

- What the blind following of analysis can reveal.
- Where the sharing of common assumptions leads.
- Where the accepted wisdom points us.
- What the acceptance of unfit rules gives us.

The current methods for developing strategy will not deliver progress of the magnitude and speed required. Researchers and academic authorities in the fields of science have examined a broad set of narrow domains and established frameworks and formulae that abstract from the complexity to define solutions to very precise problems. Given the concerted effort of scientists, particularly since the Renaissance, the number and diversity of these models of the world provide a rich body of theory and knowledge in their attempt to explain our world. Despite, or perhaps because of, this investment, scientists have been ready to make other leaps of thought in the scientific domain. Their latest theories – quantum mechanics and the uncertainty principle, chaos theory and synchronicity[1] – question the principles that underpinned previous understanding. While new answers are being developed and new methods too, perhaps one of the most significant lessons is that we have accepted models as if they were fact. This was never the intention of the inventors of the models. The inventors of the models understood the limitations of their models just as most of today's elite within the scientific research and academic community understand this. However, somewhere in the common use of these models, this was forgotten and we came to respect the models as if they were the answer. In the field of strategy, we have not had a modern Renaissance and so we do not have the richness or diversity of models to explain the world. However, the models we do have are taken literally and have resulted in narrow and dangerous strategies. These strategies lead us to wage unnecessary wars, destroy the environment and over-compete. The breakthroughs in strategic thinking since then have taken a more scientific approach in that they have picked narrower domain and produced models to address that narrow domain. Unfortunately, given the lack of investment in developing strategic thought, there have been too few breakthroughs in comparison to other fields and so we are not well equipped to formulate strategy to deal with the complex series of growing and interconnected factors facing us today. As I said earlier, the progress made in the fields of science has not been matched by that made in the fields of strategy and so we risk squandering the gains made by scientists.

ANALYSIS AND OVER-ANALYSIS: THE OVER-DEPENDENCE ON ANALYSIS

Analysis is an essential ingredient for approaching problems and providing the basis for strategy formulation, but it is only one element of what is required. Strategies based solely on analysis may be viable if they are based on superior analysis, but they will still be incomplete.

Superior analysis would be based on the use of restricted data, formulae or frameworks (restricted because they are not generally available). Since the analytic method for strategy formulation most often uses generally available information and standard analytic methods and techniques, it cannot provide distinctive answers. By using an approach that is simple, well-trodden and linear, such analytic strategies rely on the inferiority of others' analysis or the incompetence of others to follow the well-trodden path. Such strategies are 'negative' because of their reliance on others' failure.

The effect of strategies based on superior analysis is eroded once the gap narrows between the superior analysis and the rest. This gap is being eroded at an unprecedented rate due to a number of factors, including: advances in technology, as a result of which many can produce good spreadsheet models; education, as many are trained to analyse; access to information – many can access information using the internet and other public databases; and mercenaries, since many can afford consultants to analyse for them and to reveal what others are doing.

We may be able to rely on the incompetence of others for a long time. However, if we become dependent on this, we stop challenging ourselves, we ignore possibilities and ultimately we stop growing. We make ourselves unfit to survive.

Analysis is an important element of strategy, but unfortunately we have been building the mainstream culture and beliefs of our society on it. As a result, we have also reached simplistic conclusions and have accepted these simplistic answers as the formulae for success. Even more unfortunately, we have come to rely on these formulae.

SELF-LIMITING METHODS

In a study of over 2,000 scientists throughout history, it was found that the most respected scientists explored widely around their subject, thought creatively and imaginatively, and produced huge numbers of pieces of thought of variable quality. Mozart produced over 600 pieces of music, Einstein published around 250 papers, Leonardo da Vinci's notebook was some 13,000 pages long and Thomas Edison held 1,093 patents. Einstein is famously quoted as saying that whereas most people stop when they have found the needle in the haystack, he would search the entire haystack to look for all possible needles.[2]

The analytic method finds a strong following because of its very nature: it breaks down a problem into manageable pieces. It then focuses on the parts rather than the whole. This has proven to be a sound method in the discovery process for examining phenomena. However, the reasons for acceptance of this method are often based on an unconscious acceptance of our own gaps and inadequacies. There are three significant gaps.

The Methods and Concepts Gap

The first question analysts seem to avoid is: Do we have adequate methods and conceptual frameworks in our toolkit to enable us formulate good strategy? For analysis to be useful we need to be clear on the adequacy of the methods for analysing the different elements at play in a situation and the adequacy of the frameworks to enable us to step back from the situation by translating it into concepts. We pretend that we do and give too much enphasis to what can only be a limited answer from limited methods and concepts. Our existing approaches to strategic analysis are based on the false notion that the sum of the parts will equal the whole. This notion is false in assuming that the world is sufficiently well understood to assemble it from components. The known and uncontrollable factors are far too numerous and there is no easily understood method for dealing with them. Chaos theory is too nascent to provide an answer.

The Ideas Gap

The next question analysts seem to avoid is: Have we adequately explored the field and challenged our world-view? Most analysts will only be able to deal with a limited set of ideas. So, it is natural to accept a system that does not expose this weakness. People lack the time and, more importantly, the courage to explore the intangible and unknown. Instead, they make it tangible, known and, in order to be able to deal with it, small.

The Leadership Gap

Other key questions analysts seem to avoid are: Do we have the leaders for the job? Can we execute our plans? Big ventures and big adventures require visionaries, charismatic leaders and controversial thinkers. Such qualities are rare. So instead, many leaders focus on those things that do not require vision (we call it pragmatism), that do not require personality (we call them reliable), that do not require originality (we call it consensus management or team work) and that do not require courage (we call it risk management). For this pattern to be broken, we need awareness of what we do and why. We must accept that we are using limited methods that achieve limited results because they give us results we can cope with.

SELF-LIMITING TECHNIQUES

The techniques that delivered the innovations and break-throughs of the past are unlikely to deliver the breakthroughs of tomorrow. The popularisation of these techniques leads to mass adoption and thus to mass common results and therefore a lack of uniqueness. In the pharmaceutical industry, the cost of bringing a new medicine to market in the early 21st century was estimated to be as high as $0.8 to 1.7 billion. However, while pharmaceutical R&D expenditure had grown by 20 per cent each year, the number of new chemical entities launched had declined by 30 per cent. The US Food and Drug Administration attributed this to a number of causes, of which one of the most critical was that developers of medicines relied on the tools of the 20th century to make advances required in the 21st century. Their conclusion was that if biomedical science was to deliver on its promise, scientific creativity and effort must focus on improving the medical product development process itself. This problem afflicts our strategies in other fields including military strategy, corporate strategy and personal strategy.[3]

Preparing a strategy for mass adoption has required a distilling and focusing of the logical and creative process of strategy formulation. This focusing has created its own process and this process is flawed in many ways. The principle flaws are:

1 *Over-Focus on Analysis* The main method is the use of 2-by-2 matrices. We analyse things that can be easily analysed: cost vs. profit, growth vs. share, number of engineers vs. overall graduates, number of people vs. water supply. Strategy of this type is a flawed accounting process as it usually involves analysis of the past to find the future. Good accountants of course know that analysis of the past can only tell you about the past. At best, it may provide you with some questions to ask about today's situation. This method avoids creativity and holistic thinking.

2 Over-Focus on Numbers The main emphasis is on size. We look at numbers that are easy to look at: the value of tangible assets, size of profits, the GDP per capita, the numbers of tanks, the stock-pile of arms. This method ignores people, their passions and their aspirations.

3 Over-Focus on Forecasting The main method is to extrapolate results by using modelling techniques. We project the past and assume the conclusions are valid. We assume we can project manufacturing output, revenue, demand, the weather, peace and other factors in a similar way. This method ignores other more complex variables and assumes a closed loop.

4 Over-Focus on the Near Term The overwhelming motivation is to deliver short-term results. We focus on things that are close enough for us to feel comfortable. For governments, this means concentrating on the election period, for corporations, on meeting the quarterly results requirement, while for individuals the imperatives are increasingly set by the regular glossy media. This method destroys human potential by focusing it on quick results.

5 Over-Focus on the Parts The main method is categorisation or segmentation. We categorise things that make it easier for us to grasp concepts: customers, people, enemies. We put them into income bands, social class, religious groups, ethnic types and education levels. This method ignores human behaviour by over-simplifying

6 *Over-Focus on What We Have* The main method is to take an inventory. We do this simplistically using two techniques: firstly, strength and weakness analysis and, more recently, in the corporate world, core competency theory. This method avoids considering what we could have.

7 *Over-Focus on Competing* The main method is that of competitive strategy. We focus on those that we wish to beat: military competitive strategy, corporate competitive strategy, personal competitive strategy. This method harks back to a past of ignorance and/or limited means and makes us fight over assets and resources.

Again, for this pattern to be broken we need awareness of what we do and why. We must accept that we are enshrining limiting techniques and that this is leading to inferior answers.

The emphasis of our strategic processes has become a focus on things we can all do: an opium of equality. We restrict the scope of our efforts so that all of our brethren can participate and this effort reduces everything to a lower common denominator. The resulting sense of equality – amongst brethren of corporate strategists, brethren of militarists, brethren of scientists – avoids tough explorations beyond the norms of their brotherhood.

THE IMPLICATIONS OF FLAWED STRATEGIC METHOD

We have become accustomed to the use of might. Power kills and absolute power kills absolutely. This is the message of one of the most comprehensive studies of 'democide', genocide and mass murder conducted by regimes. R. J. Rummel calculates that nearly 170 million people have been killed by governments. In each case, as the arbitrary power of a regime increases massively, that is, as we move from democratic through authoritarian to totalitarian regimes, the amount of killing jumps by huge multiples. Such regimes use the most basic of strategies to achieve their ends.[4]

The constant push of flawed strategic methods has left us with little contrary thought on strategic method. The resulting strategies are shallow and flawed in concept. However, a more subtle and far more dangerous shift has also taken place: leaders in government, business and communities have reached inappropriate conclusions about what constitutes the 'right' strategy. Many of today's strategies are flawed because they:

Over-Rely on Overwhelming through Strength Our military, corporate and personal strategies too often seek to 'take the land, not the mind'. As a result, we move too quickly to armaments-based war.

Over-Rely on Closed Information Systems and Filters to Keep Control Governments, corporations and teams often create self-perpetuating beliefs and filter dissenting voices in order to maintain control. The beliefs and actions that arise are called patriotism, the XYZ Company Way, culture or norms. These ways can unite, focus and create effective patterns of behaviour. They can also solidify and exclude change. As a result, we come to believe our own propaganda.

Over-Rely on Experts The practice of asking an expert for the answer has begun to stop us thinking for ourselves. An expert is someone who simulates a narrow domain of the real world. His expertise rests on having data and knowledge of his domain. The most advanced state for an expert is insight. Experts are habitually inclined to reject new ideas because they are not yet part of the world that an expert studies.

Experts lag behind the real world because they are not subject to the pressures of the world they study. As such, they are followers, solidifying what happens in the real world into knowledge. They hold the same assumptions as the narrow slice of the real world they study, only more rigidly, and are incapable of wisdom or strategy. To be wise and strategic, they would have to reject the basis of their expertise, they would have to challenge assumptions, risk unpopularity and go beyond the boundaries of their expertise, thereby risking their past success. Individuals who have the label of expert sometimes do this, but when they do they are no longer acting as experts.

Over-Rely on the Utilisation of Assets and the Strengthening of our Inherited Resources Strategy departments begin with inventories of their institution's assets and competencies and apply these to situations. The implicit assumption is to fit what we have to the situation that confronts us. The result is to limit what we do by what we have. These strategies are often called 'core competency' strategies. As a result, we limit the imagination, strategy and outcome to seeing only a battle between existing, often inherited, assets.

Over-Rely on the Defence of an Existing Position Our strategies seek to protect rather than expand. Such 'clinging' strategies account for the huge numbers of companies in tier 2 and 3 positions in so many industries who have no hope of advancing in their sector and have no intention of exiting. As a result, we create stagnation.

Over-Rely on Finite Resource Theory Such strategies seek to exploit situations based on the view that resources, and therefore choices, are limited. As a result, strategy becomes a game of prioritisation and resource allocation.

These flaws in thinking apply to governments, corporations, investors, communities and individuals. Our strategies are creating a system that cannot survive.

THE FAILURE OF STRATEGY IS SYSTEMIC

In the early 21st century, systemic failures afflicted all aspects of our world:

- 11 per cent of all bird species, 25 per cent of mammals, and 34 per cent of fish were in danger of extinction.
- The Amazon Rainforest was vanishing at 3 times the rate it was in 1994; 20 per cent of the it had already been obliterated. The deforestation rate was 78 million acres per year and 80 per cent of the ancient forests had already been destroyed.
- Every year US industries release at least 2.4 billion lb of chemicals into the atmosphere.
- From the stock market value highs of March 2000 to October 2002, the value of stocks fell by $7.5 trillion from the fixed and wireless telecommunications, telecom equipment, broader technology and media industries.
- US Attorney General, Elliott Spitzer, brought cases against the major American industries over a period of four years (2000–2004) – investment banking, commercial banking, mutual funds, insurance and pharmaceuticals and healthcare – that had underpinned the growth of the US stock market and corporate strength all around the world for the previous 25 years.[4]

THE FAILURE OF CORPORATIONS TO DELIVER
SUPERIOR VALUE

At the turn of the 20th century, most industries consisted of a few large corporations that dominated the industry and a large number of unprofitable companies who struggled to survive but refused to exit the industry. The system failed to force substantial consolidation, to enable innovation to create new positions and new value, or to pressure the weakest into collapsing and withdrawing. Indeed, the system supported the strugglers by enabling refinancing of unprofitable pursuits. Hence we had too many companies in the semi-conductor, communications–technology, telecommunications services, banking and insurance, and consumer electronics sectors all merely surviving.

The roots of failure to create value lie inside the corporations and in the wider capital system that supports them. Few companies pursue strategies: most pursue an idea. The idea is usually someone else's idea and this original idea is pursued by many well beyond its usefulness. Cost reduction, mergers and acquisitions, business process re-engineering and Six Sigma are all examples of packaged solutions offered as substitutes for innovating. They can all add value but the relative value necessarily diminishes over time.

There is a pattern to the focus of leaders. The focus of leaders shifts from inside – cost, operations, people – to outside – markets, geographies, competitors – depending upon the swing of fortune. The recorder and dictator of that swing is the stock market.

The stock market has been critical to enabling corporations to raise capital in order to pursue their strategies. However, without intending to, we have promoted the stock market to a position well beyond its design. It has now become trading hall, accountant, judge and jury. Rather than acting as the facilitator of the efficient flow of capital, it has become the ultimate measure of our effectiveness. A set of implicit 'rules' has grown up around it: to reward inefficiency by enabling companies to grow too big, even if this results in management diseconomies; to reward the pursuit of transactions such that companies follow cycles of consolidation and deconsolidation; to reward ineffective behaviour by focusing management on the short-term delivery of results; and, through the pressure to deliver returns, focusing management on exploiting loop-holes. Those that play the game well become the heroes. Real strategy is subjugated to game playing, herd behaviour and rule bending.

The system has become an ideology. That is, we have formed an ideological belief in the system as it exists today. As a result, our questioning of the system at the most senior levels is inadequate and we seek to enforce the system on others. The 'nature' of personal histories, contexts, races and cultures are denied and the adoption of the system is encouraged blindly. Instead of the system facilitating our growth, entrepreneurial risk-taking and wealth creation, it becomes the end in itself.

Both the management approach to strategy, and the wider capital system within which management operates, needs to be re-thought to return to truer measures of value creation.

THE FAILURE OF INVESTORS TO SPUR WEALTH CREATION

At the turn of the 20th century, we had all but declared the victory of stock market-driven capitalism. Then the equity market collapse of 2000 threw the world into a recession that wiped trillions off the capital markets, pension funds and savings plans of the most capitalised economies. This collapse was shortly followed by a series of frauds and bad decisions, and included much lauded, and sometimes much respected, companies such as Worldcom, Enron and Tyco shaking first confidence in the US stock markets and then those of other developed countries. The collapse revealed much, including flaws in investor strategies and flaws in the working of stock markets themselves.

In relation to capital markets, the market was shown to be underpinned by systemic flaws. These flaws were evident in the reporting of financial results; in the incentives given to and lack of independence of investment research; in the compensation of executives; and in the governance of companies.

With regard to the largest institutional investors, the returns delivered by these investors during the growth of the market were revealed to be a result of the growth of the market rather than the outcome of clever investment strategies. The strategies of the large institutional investor, on whom depends the value of savings, pensions and insurances, was shown to be based on a flawed way, or system, of doing business.

These flaws lay in investment strategies based on tracking indices rather than more discriminative investing; failure to form a distinctive view of the basis of investments resulting from an over-dependence on unimaginative external research; pacifism towards corporate performance and an unwillingness and inability to cause change in poorly performing corporations; and investment instruments and products that were suited to growing markets but unable to benefit from falling or volatile markets. As if to prove the validity of the flaws, a new breed of investor emerged to seize the opportunities: the hedge fund or 'alternative' investor. Over time, this class of investor would also bloat, lose distinctiveness and split into the fit and the unfit.

Again, both the basic workings of the market and the approach to investing need to be re-thought to enable creation of greater value.

THE FAILURE OF GOVERNMENT TO CREATE PEACE, PROSPERITY AND FREEDOM

At the turn of the 20th century, the West had accepted the triumph of democracy and Western-style capitalism. It expected world peace as a result. This view was thrown into question by the September 11th attack on the US. The ensuing war on Afghanistan, followed by the continued search for the aggressors, also shook the notion that peace and stability had been achieved. The way that the US conducted the subsequent war on Iraq then destabilised the notion of a united allied front. What continued to catch world attention was how easy it had been to win the war but how difficult it was to secure peace. The re-stated ambition of freedom for the Iraqi people seemed elusive and the wider ambition of peace in the Middle East seemed to remain beyond the strategy of world leaders.

In the first few years of the 21st century, as Western markets collapsed and swung wildly up and down amidst loss of confidence and fraud, China continued to execute an effective plan to achieve prosperity. China became the world's fastest growing market, the most attractive destination for capital and the most attractive residence for corporations failing to find growth elsewhere. For the high potential developing economies of the world, such as India, Brazil and Russia, China began to look like an attractive alternative to Western-style capitalist democracy as a way of creating prosperity.

Systemic flaws in the strategies of the world's most modernised nations were shown by: the advocacy of capitalism from an ideological perspective rather than from the perspective of promoting prosperity; the belief that we should impose our ideas on others, rather than just our products and services (the globalisation of ideas and ideologies); the assumption that democracy is appropriate for all countries, regardless of their readiness and without due consideration to the institutions required to establish freedoms; and the belief that supremacy allows social engineering on a grand scale.

At the end of the Second World War, a number of super- and cross-national entities were established with the dream of learning the lessons of the failure of nations in containing global aggressors and establishing lasting peace. Institutions such as the UN, World Bank and the IMF had important political and economic mandates beyond nation states. By the early 21st century, it was clear that these institutions were often at odds with the interests of America as the sole superpower and did not have the ability to discharge their mandates. It also became more and more questionable what the role of a supranational power was in a world where one country felt it had the ability to execute its aims on a global basis.

The assumptions, tools and strategies of governments will need to be rethought to deliver peace, prosperity and freedom.

THE PERSONAL FAILURE TO CREATE BALANCE

As the 20th century drew to a close, the world was going through a rise in optimism based on a technology boom that drove the paper value of individuals' wealth to unprecedented levels. Policy makers and their advisors spoke of the 'digital divide', a world of technology 'haves' and 'have-nots', as the critical issue for enabling an even greater number to participate in the new wealth and for unlocking personal freedom. The massive opportunity to create personal wealth led people to break the habit of avoiding risk. They were more prepared to become entrepreneurs. Many were prepared to leave secure jobs in large corporations, stop working in major cities and embrace new remuneration schemes. The response from corporations, governments and 'experts' was to herald a new era of personal balance. This initiative died away as soon as the stock market bubble burst and the world returned quickly to the habits of old. This loss of confidence was accentuated by unemployment, wars and the loss of stock market dependent wealth.

The surface rippled by the technology boom had deeper roots. The brief appearance of a new way of living, briefly created by the technology boom, reveals more. The deeper roots reveal dissatisfaction with mundane existences and a yearning for something more. This yearning is instilled in our various cultures and is characterised by the outward search – followed by 'Western' cultures – and the inward search – pursued by 'Eastern' cultures. In the early part of the 21st century, with global communication and unprecedented amounts of information available to people both paths were available to Humankind.

The West had made enormous strides in achieving its outward quest and was set to continue to break new external boundaries. Each boundary broken – space, biology, computing, material science – unlocked more and more economic value. Of course, every boundary that was broken revealed a new boundary. More importantly, there was no answer to the fundamental questions 'Who am I?' and 'Why am I here?'

The East had also made enormous strides in achieving its quest of breaking new internal boundaries. Each boundary broken – metaphysics, meditation, lucid dreams, physio-emotional control, energy transmission – unlocked more and more personal value. Of course, every barrier broken had to be broken individually: economies had not been achieved in the transfer of these breakthroughs and the methods were not 'scaleable', that is, they were not easily transferable to a large mass of the population. More importantly, there was inadequate generation of economic value and prosperity and so the East had become impoverished in this quest.

Neither the West nor the East had found the balance. Neither great pioneering scientific crusade of conquest nor the great journey for inner truth had found peace, prosperity and freedom for society. In addition, large sections of the world's population, in particular most of Africa and many parts of Latin America, have achieved neither the outer nor the inner conquests.

The global organised religions of Christianity, Islam, Buddhism and Hinduism, had failed to deliver personal peace to mass populations, or prosperity to those that lived in faith but lacked the benefits of scientific and technological advances. Nor had they established liberty for those that lacked human institutions such as democracy. This failure was as much a failure of the priests, mullahs and gurus as it was of the individual.

The approaches and methods, not just of societies but also of individuals, will need to be rethought if balance is to be achieved.

THE FRUITS OF OUR STRATEGIES: HUGE ADVANCEMENT AND HUGE DISRUPTION

The strategies in our history have succeeded in delivering an enormous amount of actual value and an enormous amount of potential value. The actual and potential value is inherent in phenomena such as the Seven Shaping Phenomena, described in the opening chapter. The actual value comes from the continual and inexorable breaking of barriers to performance; the unprecedented mass of information, media and communication available to us; the compression of time, distance and access; the unlocking of creativity from every corner of the world; the connectivity of the world's people through multiple global systems; the rise of fixed positions; and the presence of overwhelming latent power. The potential or unrealised value results from the same phenomena. Every achievement has placed us in a position to unlock even greater value now or, if our strategies are inadequate, to stall or destroy value. For every achievement, there is a counter-balancing force that can result in stagnation or destruction.

The failure of the strategies of today's institutions, particularly governments, corporations and communities, is the biggest obstacle to the realisation of our potential. As we have already discussed, the failing systems include corporations, who have failed to deliver superior returns from the exploitation of the world's resources; investors, who have failed to spur adequate wealth creation from our invested capital; governments, who have failed to deliver peace, prosperity and freedom; empires and supra- and cross-national entities, who have failed to deliver value beyond the nation state; communities, who have failed to deliver peace, prosperity and respect of mutual rights; religions, who have failed to deliver a sufficient number of enlightened beings able to foster the love and compassion required to address the failings of other systems; and finally, individuals, who have failed to deliver themselves from a life that is unbalanced by fear and greed.

Each of the institutional systems considered above is subjected to two key negative forces – predatory forces and accidental or chaotic forces – that challenge their ability to deliver intended outcomes. These result in three types of negative reactions: apathy and complacency (the unwillingness to change); self-destructive behaviour (the internal power struggle between people and between factions); and incompetent or flawed action (the poor execution of change). The cumulative impact of these reactions is to make the system unfit to survive. The system therefore becomes irrelevant.

Our systems of government, corporation, investing, supra-government bodies, community and individual are in danger of losing their relevance and their ability to unlock the potential that previous strategies have left us. As systems lose their relevance, a gap is created, and alternative systems arrive to displace previously established ones: revolutionaries seek to displace dictators; hedge funds seek to displace mutual funds; hostile take-overs arrive to displace complacent under-performing companies; and diseases strike our bodies and minds once we fall out of the 'fit zone'. As alternative systems strive to establish themselves, the result is an escalating tension with the systems they seek to replace. This fight for survival results in either a recalibration of the established systems or a destruction of them. This is natural and to be expected.

Systems that are less fit to survive will inevitably give way to those that are fitter. This must apply to governments, corporations, investing institutions, cross-government coalition entities, supra-government entities, communities, religions and individuals. To sustain power beyond this natural turn of events requires an abuse of the position of the system in a society – a rogue system. Rogue systems come in many forms, including superpowers and empires that impose themselves on others without popular support from the international community and so lose their moral high ground; dictators who ruthlessly crush freedom-fighters; regulators that allow predatory corporations and devious investing behaviour to survive; governments that protect national industries to avoid the political pain of restructuring; and healthcare establishments that institutionalise bad life styles through cure at the expense of prevention.

ALTERNATIVE SYSTEMS

Today's alternative systems are slowly fighting the established systems in a war for survival and ultimately for domination.

Alternative Corporations These corporations use new disruptive technologies, converge existing technologies, use online distribution models and build superscale manufacturing or distribution networks to threaten the existing corporations. At the beginning of the 21st century, the alternative corporate systems included Nokia, Dell, e-Bay, China's growing electronics companies, India's Bangalore outsourcing valley and the Aids foundations of major philanthropists as they begin to challenge the way medicines were priced and distributed.

Alternative Investing Models These deliver superior returns through products that are more capable of dealing with recession, uncertainty and volatility as well as growth. At the beginning of the 21st century, the alternative investing systems were headed by the hedge funds with the flexibility and speed to exploit change. They went by unfamiliar names such as Maverick, Citadel and Fortress, the best of whom were showing the promise of changing the face of investing.

Alternative Government Models These new systems of

government promise to deliver better peace and prosperity than existing models, with the promise of freedom to follow. At the beginning of the 21st century, the alternative government model was that of the Chinese, with its delivery of managed growth, wealth creation, modernisation and prosperity for its people.

Alternative Inter-Governmental Coalitions These coalitions offer a faster and more effective solution to the political stalemates suffered by institutions such as the UN, the IMF and the World Bank, and act as a counter-balance to the almost all-pervasive powerful political institution that is America. The coalitions included bilateral and multi-lateral trade agreements, regional trading blocs and various diverse private philanthropist-initiated institutions.

Alternative Communities These new communities provide greater affinity and rewards for members. At the beginning of the 21st century, alternative communities included a multitude of internet-based ones focused on the most fundamental human pursuits, such as games, education, health, sport, charity and violence.

Alternative Faiths Such faiths and methods offer faster progress towards self-realisation. In the middle of the 20th century, Americans were the biggest seekers of finding a more meaningful 'Way' in the world. The older spiritual cultures sent gurus, healers and teachers to create new age movements in America. They were a mixed crowd of the competent and incompetent, shy and publicity-seeking, charlatans and deeply profound. Some persisted, some changed and some were persecuted. However, over a period of two decades, America was left with the world's greatest concentration of yoga, t'ai chi,

Zen, acupuncture, reiki and healing methods outside the countries of origin. At the beginning of the 21st century, the alternatives continued to be formally incorporated into society with health clubs, corporations, doctors and hospitals offering the techniques without the philosophy. The individual had begun to seek to fill the gap left by the formal and collective worship-based models of religion which provided inadequate answers to science, politics, personal development and the afflictions of the world through following alternative methods and faiths.

Alternative Personal Development and Balance This pursuit had become a huge industry. The growth of the self-development industry had benefited from the rise in individualism, personalisation and the decline in loyalty to existing institutions or methods. Alternative diets and health regimes, education programmes, retreats, classes and courses are all part of this growth area.

Given the huge achievements and capabilities of Man, we are now at a time of great potential. The potential gives us the opportunity to make a discontinuous change in a positive or negative direction. Given the rise of alternative systems that challenge the status quo, we can also expect a power struggle between the existing systems and the new ones.

Strategies will need to be formulated to reshape the established systems if they are to be part of the way ahead. Such strategies will be different from the past in the way they apply power, purpose and principle. The current definitions will be challenged: power will no longer mean the enforcing of will over others; purpose will no longer mean merely the pursuit of personal ambitions; and principle will no longer be defined at a level that separates us based on our politics, culture, religion or geography. The new definitions will emerge through the remainder of this work. In the next chapter, we will examine the nature of power, purpose and principle in strategy.

THE BOOK OF POWER, PURPOSE AND PRINCIPLE

'To judge who will succeed, assess who has power, who has purpose and who has principle. It is at the intersections of these three that strategies are played out and the struggle takes place.'

The Book of Power, Purpose and Principle

'A STREAM OF CONSCIOUSNESS'

Is it possible to develop effective strategy in the face of enormous challenges, such as the seven we described in the opening chapter of this work? What kind of strategy is required to succeed? Is there such a thing as a sustainable strategy or sustainable competitive advantage? Is there something fundamental about strategy that transcends the field of application? That is, can we be generally strategic or can we be strategic only in a specific field such as that of corporate strategy, government strategy, investing strategy and personal strategy? Can we separate strategy from the individual? In this chapter, we will examine these and other fundamental questions.

In conducting an examination of strategy, it is important to realise that, at its heart, strategy is about the interaction of the personal with the impersonal. Since strategies are formulated by individuals, they are highly personal. Since they are intended to affect others, their domain of operation is outside the person. This ignores, of course, the philosophical argument that everything is personal since everything arises from our own perception. It also ignores the counter-philosophical argument that there is a reality independent of the individual. We will be simplistic about these questions in our purpose of examining the nature of strategy.

In our examination of strategy, we will need to recognise that a number of objects are in play. The most critical objects are the strategist, the target of the strategy and the situation in which strategy will be conducted. These objects can be viewed as physical objects and also as intangible objects: the intangible elements are the power, purpose and principle of the people involved. In other words, strategy is also about individuals seeking to assert their world view on others and, in doing so, they may use weapons such as money, armies and media.

Modern strategic doctrine mostly fails to include the person and his aims in the strategic framework. Lip service is paid to the notions of vision, mission and objectives. This makes strategy highly impersonal. Once we accept the highly personal nature of strategy, we realise that it can only be as good as the strategist. Modern strategic doctrine has too often avoided this issue by focusing on the strategic process. This takes accountability out of strategy by making strategy merely the outcome of a process rather than a personal statement about what to do. Regardless of the process, strategies are either fit for the situation and the environment or they are not. Once we accept the impersonal context within which strategy is to be conducted, we realise that strategy is closely linked to the environment within which it is conducted.

To bring us back to the personal and impersonal

fundamentals of strategy, we will explore strategy through an examination of the following nine areas:

1   The nature of strategy
2   The role of power, purpose and principle
3   The characteristics of the strategist
4   The importance of awareness
5   The role of the winning ambition
6   The mentality of being beyond winning
7   The nature of the ruling syndrome
8   Results and the role of view, position and influence
9   The importance of mastery and self-mastery

With regard to the personal nature of strategy: we will assert that the path to forming good strategy is intensely personal and we will aim to show that it cannot be achieved without a highly developed individual. The highly developed individual would have achieved 'maturity' through the pursuit of a varied and rigorous path, with the aim of relentlessly developing himself and his awareness of the world. The diversionary nature of modern strategic thinking, focused on simplistic processes, frameworks and formulae, has led us to ignore this. Maturity is one of the most important bases of strategy. For simplicity, we will define three states of maturity. The basic state we will call the Strategist, the next, the Master Strategist and the ultimate, the Enlightened Strategist. The path to forming good strategy is largely impersonal and we will aim to show that the fit strategist is merely the one who happens to be fit for the environment.

A word on method for this chapter. Contemplation is more important than the formula that we have been given in the past. So, the approach will be to preface each of the nine areas with some of the key questions that may help us to understand the subject. Thereafter, you will see that what follows is closer to a 'stream of consciousness' than an exploration of the subject through hypothesis, counter-point, reference to others, case study, formula or framework.[1] In Chapter four we will examine some of the key aspects discussed in this chapter in more detail.

1 STRATEGY

The fundamental questions to contemplate include:

- *What is strategy and what do we mean by differentiation?*
- *Is there such a thing as the one right strategy?*
- *What is the role of analysis and imagination in strategy?*

1 Strategy is fundamentally about difference. Strategy therefore denies equality, striving for sameness and belief in the one answer.

2 Difference requires leaps beyond what others can grasp.

3 Strategy recognises the huge diversity of the world and the resulting infinite possibilities, and chooses paths that others cannot follow.

4 Strategic thought is in opposition to the form of rational thought that assumes a sequential, simplistic, mathematical approach that leads to one answer.

5 Strategy based on superior analysis can lead to short-term successes and should be a first step. It is a tactic rather than a strategy.

6 Analysis focuses on the part rather than the whole. The analyst is required to analyse the parts. The strategist is required to see the pattern.

7 Strategy is about systems of people and objects, and the interaction in and between hierarchies of systems.

8 Strategy is about results involving, but never limited by, people.

9 Strategies are destroyed when they become fads. Plagiarism destroys strategies and absolute plagiarism destroys strategies absolutely.

2 POWER, PURPOSE AND PRINCIPLE

The fundamental questions to contemplate include:

- *What are the key intangibles that are present in any situation?*
- *What role do emotions play in strategy?*
- *What is the difference between the Master Strategist and others in this regard?*

1   To judge who will succeed assess who has power, who has purpose and who has principle. It is at the intersections of these three that strategies are played out and the struggle takes place. It is at the centre of all three that Master Strategists and Enlightened Strategists operate.

2   At the intersection of power and principle is the force that is driven by belief in itself and by belief that 'right' is on its side.

3   At the intersection of power and purpose is might exerting itself to gain more might.

4   At the intersection of purpose and principle is the struggle between determined forces with self-belief but without the power to execute.

5   All such strategies are driven by emotions. Peace can only be achieved once these emotions have been conquered.

6   At the intersection of power, purpose and principle there are all three: there is determined might and right. The Master Strategist operates at the intersection of power, purpose and principle. Hence he prevails.

7   The Enlightened Strategist is one who can create and combine superior power, purpose and principle. He has superior power, such that others accept that he can win

so he has no need to exercise power. He has superior purpose, such that others accept his purpose. He has the principles that lead others to accept his authority.

8   So, at the intersection of power, purpose and principle there is the absence of power, purpose and principle. The Enlightened Strategist operates in this void.

3 THE STRATEGIST

The fundamental questions to contemplate include:

- *What is the role of the strategist in strategy?*
- *What are the critical characteristics of the strategist?*
- *How do we judge whether a strategy is superior?*

1 The Strategist is open, deliberate and measured. Being open enables influence to enter. Being deliberate enables choice. Being measured enables controlled action.

2 There is no progress before self-progress; you cannot master strategy until you master yourself.

3 To be a strategist one must have the courage to question oneself, the will to persevere, the training to know how to ask, the mentoring to be effective, the support to discharge other responsibilities and the ability to see the need to do all of this.

4 Master Strategists create 'Golden Periods' when their chosen vehicles – personal, organisational, national or imperial – prevail.

5 These Golden Periods die when the strategy merely becomes an idea that the multitude can follow.

6 The same elements are present. The superior strategist constructs them into a superior form. Superior because it is more efficient and effective for any given purpose.

7 The Master Strategist only pursues ideas and purposes of the highest order. The highest order is judged by its fit to three simple principles: its ability to rise above contending positions, to take whole and to act with the flow.

8 At any point in time, the Master Strategist may remain still, initiate, engage or destroy. The three principles of

rising above, taking whole and acting with the flow remain.

9   Positive results require a spirit of compassion. When situations are approached in a spirit of self-interest, negative results are more likely. The Master Strategist is one who has cultivated compassion in himself if he is to cultivate peace, prosperity and freedom in others.

10   The strategic state of an entity is superior to the strategist of that entity. In the strategic state, the body of the entity has capability, readiness and spontaneity. The task of the Master Strategist is to create a strategic entity.

11   There is no such thing as an outcome in an absolute sense. Outcome is a transitory state and, as such, is simply a milestone in a flow of events. Master Strategists see the flow of events and influence the flow.

4 AWARENESS

The fundamental questions to contemplate include:

- *What do we have to understand to formulate good strategy?*
- *What understanding is required to go beyond good strategy?*
- *Where does this increasing understanding lead us?*

1   The good strategist sees his adversary and sees the conflict. The excellent strategist sees the situation of both himself and his adversary. The superior strategist detaches himself from his adversary to see the wider environment of the situation and sees how he and his adversary fit.

2   The Master Strategist observes only the situation with no attachment to it, you or himself and understands how the game can be played. For the Enlightened Strategist there is no situation, there is a flow of situations.

3   Most actions are undertaken without seeing or understanding; without seeing or understanding the situation, the adversary or oneself. Most protagonists engage in conflict without seeing or understanding. The quality of a strategy is a function of how well the strategist sees and understands.

4   The Enlightened Strategist does not need to engage. For the rest 'seeing' and understanding are critical to successfully engaging.

5   Individuals, and organisations, are subject to cause and effect. To find balance we must not be at the extreme ends of cause and effect: we must not over- or under-react. This is achieved when we control the causes and the effects on us. This is possible through negation of

cause and effect.

6   Assimilation of cause and effect leads to stress. Negation of cause and effect requires detachment. 'You', 'I' and 'it' stand in the way of detachment. To achieve detachment we must develop a high quality of awareness.

7   The events in the world result from causes that we do not understand. The interrelatedness of these causes has consequences that we do not understand. Our actions cause outcomes that we do not understand. The result is chaos. A better future requires us to understand better the nature of things today.

8   Sometimes chaos appears to have order. So we think we understand what we observe.

9   In the midst of the complexity there appears to be no pattern. Stepping above the inexplicable complexity we may see a pattern. Stepping too far up, we see nothing.

10   The Master Strategist is aware of the detail and also the pattern. He sees them as a whole.

11   Success without knowledge is chance. Strategy without awareness is accident. Intentional results require awareness. Detached observation is beyond strategy.

12   Often, first we know, then we become aware and then we can observe. This is how strategists are transformed into Master Strategists and then into Enlightened Strategists.

The fundamental questions to contemplate include:

- *What does it mean to win?*
- *What are the strategies for winning?*
- *Can a position that we have won be sustained?*

The Essence of Winning

1   The way to sustain power beyond what is 'natural', that is, beyond your competency and beyond what is 'fit', is to become 'unnatural'. To become unnatural you must employ unnatural methods; these include brutality, exploitation and destruction. Unnatural actions attract unnatural responses. Ultimately, you put in place a cycle of unnatural behaviour which goes beyond your original aim and moves beyond your control.

2   Strategies that have destruction as their main aim are inferior to strategies that have winning as their main aim. If someone has to die, the winning strategy generally requires the opponent to die. Superior strategies require no contention. Such strategies are the most difficult to perceive.

3   Strategies of contention require a preparedness to kill. Killing brutalises the essence of Man. Extensive killing makes the brutalised essence numb.

4   An intelligent entity is culturally programmed to act in a winning manner. Killing the leader can kill the sustainability of the cause if the body is not autonomous, if it is not intrinsically coded with the mission and with the capability to act independently. If it is so coded, the killing merely raises the stakes and

makes winning more difficult.

5   There are five strategic paths: competition, disruption, domination, inclusion and aspiration. Competition, disruption and domination are about winning and therefore also about losing. The paths of inclusion and aspiration place us beyond winning and losing.

Competition

6   The most basic strategic path is that of competition. Sometimes we find ourselves in the battle of competition. Essentially, the battle is one for the mind. To beat the mind of the opponent requires the undermining or corrupting of the opponent's mind so that for any given situation yours is the fitter mind. Such a struggle is fraught with danger since to conquer the mind is to take the most important asset owned by the opponent.

7   The superior mind wins because it has not been corrupted into becoming inflexible, and non-adaptive. To win, you must become flexible and adaptive and create inflexibility to prevent adaptation in your opponent.

8   Firstly, reinforce his assumptions and beliefs, thereby creating inflexibility. Throw him into confusion, so that he avoids closure and prolongs the status quo, thereby losing the initiative. Thereby, you seize the initiative.

9   Secondly, put him in situations where he has to suppress his emotions, causing them to rule him. Thereby, you induce emotional responses whilst you retain superior control.

10   Present him with evidence that reveals answers quickly,

in order to encourage shallow enquiry. Cause him to switch from over-criticism to under-criticism of events, thereby causing his judgement to become impaired.

11   Undermine your opponent's ability to trust by putting into question the competency of his people, thereby causing internal dissension amongst them, inconsistency and volatility in their behaviour, and as a result reducing intimacy between them and increasing the risk of failure. Thereby, united, you cause dissension within your opponent.

12   Finally, freeze your opponent's imagination by overwhelming him not only with too much data, but also random data points that reveal no clear pattern and force him to take 'pragmatic' and practical actions. Thereby you induce 'practical' and 'pragmatic' behaviour.

13   When your opponent talks of being 'practical' and 'pragmatic', know that he lacks imagination. So, give him obvious paths to follow that lead nowhere useful and, if necessary, wait for him down those paths to subdue him.

14   The methods for corrupting the opponent's mind may be initiated by you but require the compliance of the opponent. Such strategies undermine the assumptions, beliefs and values of the opponent.

15   Strategies to beat the opponent's mind may be required to avoid destroying the opponent.

16   Strategies are corrupted by corrupting the mind. The way for corrupting your opponent's strategies is also the way in which your own strategies are corrupted.

Disruption

17   The second strategic path is one of disruption. When fighting an overwhelmingly large force, direct attack is futile. Instead, focus on disruption. Disruptions are usually ignored at conception by the overwhelmingly large.

18   Disruptions can be either one-off major events that shake the system or they can be a series of small shocks that cumulatively undermine it. The difference is in the timing of achieving the result.

19   Disruptions can be bred. Disruptions can be bred to behave like viruses that attack and undermine the performance of the target.

20   The most effective viruses will spread quickly and have origins that are difficult to track. The overwhelmingly large entity will usually attack the symptoms. When the virus is evident, it is too late to halt it without drastic steps. Drastic steps will, by definition, be disruptive to the attacker.

21   The intelligent virus will be adaptive to the situation and will learn to survive assault.

22   An overwhelmingly large protagonist can recover from a virus. To disable such a protagonist, deploy multiple viruses. Each virus must be distinct for maximum effect. In this way, the target will have to attack each one independently and will not be able to create a common defence.

23   So, overwhelmingly large opponents can be undermined by the use of disruptive viruses. The large retaliate with force, and so diversion, decoy and deception become important tactics of the disruptive strategist. The way to undermine your opponent's strategies is also the way in which your own strategies can be undermined.

24   The disruptive strategist is one who can breed disruptions. The disruptive strategist is one who can nurture, rally and direct such disruptions. The disruptive strategist is one who can design a disruption such that by its very nature, it will behave in a certain way and then with minimum nurturing he can watch it take its disruptive course. Hence the disruptive strategist remains invisible.

Domination

25   The third strategic path is one of domination. Domination results from sustaining one-sided power in relationships.

26   To establish domination requires one to possess something desirable and to share sufficient benefits to create a pattern of 'followership' from the targets.

27   To dominate, you need to possess a one-off advantage of sufficient scale to create sustainable distance between yourself and others.

28   To dominate, you need to possess a renewable advantage and invest to renew that advantage.

29   To dominate, a stagnant environment is required, so that effective competition is not created.

30   To sustain domination, targets must be willing to be dominated. The price of freedom must be too high a price to pay.

31   Domination leads to predatory behaviour, because it becomes habitual and steps are taken to sustain the power position beyond its 'natural' time. Such behaviour is 'unnatural' because it is sustained beyond the point where sufficient advantages are conferred for others to give up freedom.

32   No advantage is sustained indefinitely. Domination
      when sustained 'unnaturally' leads to rebellion.

33   Aggressive strategies of domination lead to extreme
      methods. Some such methods are effective, others are
      not. Once such a course has been taken, the
      consequences are annihilation or brutality against those
      that resist.

34   In the absence of annihilation, brutality will be required.
      In the absence of brutality, compromise and
      reconciliation will be required. In the absence of
      compromise and reconciliation, incompetence will
      prevail.

35   Action is required to achieve annihilation and brutality.
      Flawed strategy and flawed action is required to achieve
      incompetence. Master strategy is required to achieve
      reconciliation.

36   If one is not willing to bear the consequences of
      aggressive strategies of domination, one should not
      embark upon them.

37   Domination can also be achieved through wealth. The
      basis of strategy then becomes the acquisition of
      wealth. Wealth can form an effective barrier to prevent
      others gaining power. Wealth can lead to power.
      Without an effective strategy to maintain effective
      barriers to others gaining power, the power will
      dissolve. With the dissolution of power, often, the
      wealth dissolves too.

Importance of Losing

38   To understand winning, we must study failing. Our
      failures lead our enemies to make assumptions about us.
      These assumptions often embolden them and lead them

to take actions against us. The consequences of these actions can go beyond the magnitude of our initial failure and so we become vulnerable. Unchecked this leads to our downfall.

6 BEYOND WINNING

The fundamental questions to contemplate include:

- *What are the consequences of winning?*
- *Can winning be sustained?*
- *Is there something more important than winning?*

Beyond Winning and Losing

1   The Master Strategist approaches an aggressor with the knowledge that the aggression is not a conflict between himself and the self-appointed rival. The only aggression can be within himself and within the aggressor. This is a matter of self-control. If the battle for self-control has been won, there are no more aggressors and no more battles. After that, it is merely a question of execution.

2   The attitude of the strategist is that there is no such thing as failure, there is only the situation and the lesson.

3   Apart from the enlightened, no one is immune to retaliation, to cause and effect. Cause leads to effect and becomes cause.

4   The aware are aware of the 'retaliation' potential in every action and see every event as a single phenomenon within a flow of retaliations.

5   Hence, the Master Strategist is aware of the flow, the possible interventions to this flow and the possible consequences. He does not only react to the event.

6   Those whose awareness, imagination and judgement are impaired see their actions as final.

7   Hence, superior strategists calculate the costs of physical conflict carefully and understand the superiority of

winning the mind rather than beating the mind or body of the opponents.

8   You cannot effect sustainable change without changing minds.

9   To defeat others is the wrong way to think. If you rise to the highest purpose, you will be beyond contention.

10   To 'win' you may need to crush others. Although things crushed are often lost, the essence of their contention often lives on. To truly win you must deal with the essence. The essence is evident in the mind. It comprises beliefs and values amongst other things. So, to win, you will need to win your opponent's mind.

11   You must rise above the field and see the pattern, if you are to fight and win in the field.

12   To win in the field is inferior to transforming the field. Which is inferior to moving to a better field. Which is inferior to not being in the field.

13   In order not to be compelled to be on the field of battle, you need pre-emption. Foresight regarding possibilities, capabilities and intentions enables pre-emption. If you wage well the war to understand possibilities, capabilities and intentions, you may never have to go to war. Possibilities, capabilities and intentions have no substance; they are of the mind. Therefore, ultimately, the real war is of the mind.

14   Lasting strategies focus on innovations to enhance life, creating an efficient financial and reward system, establishing adaptive organisational systems, increasing influence over people's lives and creating a worthy forum in which people can apply themselves.

Inclusion

15   Strategies that unleash such potential are inclusive of others and are aspirational in nature.

16   Inclusion recognises the interrelatedness of things. Inclusive strategies require alignment. Alignment requires energy to be channelled. Channelling requires power. Power can be exercised by individuals over themselves or over each other. Since power over oneself is the more difficult of the two, men pursue power over each other. This power, by its nature, is divisive, because it seeks to create a power-wielder and a power-servant. Hence, alignment is not achieved.

17   Hence, inclusive strategies create synchronicity. Activities become coordinated and so achieve a predetermined outcome; initiatives are pursued that achieve common goals and assets merge to create synergy.

18   Entities define themselves as separate. Entities fail to behave in accordance with an understanding of the interrelatedness of all things. This failure applies to all manner of entities, including people, organisations and countries.

19   Inclusive strategies fail because of the inability of many entities to move as one and adapt adequately to changing circumstances. The failure is one of the direction in which energy is applied. Therefore, the failure is one of the application of power. Therefore, the failure is one of strategy

Aspiration

20   To achieve results without conflict requires an aspirational approach. Aspiration-based strategies recognise

the huge diversity of potential paths and recognise that there is no need for each of us to follow the same path.

21 Hence the Master Strategist inspires people to innovate, improve, grow, explore, change and influence.

22 Great strategies change people and unlock their energy.

23 Strategists channel resources to achieve their purpose. The effective strategist channels energy to achieve purpose. The superior strategist unlocks energy so that it achieves purpose. The Master Strategist unlocks energy, fills it with superior principle, helps it find purpose and makes it powerful.

Beyond Enmity

24 The Enlightened Strategist is beyond enmity. The Master Strategist does not confer lightly the status of enemy on anyone.

25 Those that can be defeated easily are not enemies, they are merely sparring partners. Those that can be defeated with some effort are opponents. Enemies are wise. In their wisdom they also seek to rise above contending positions, take whole and act with the flow.

26 Distinguish between enemies, opponents and sparring partners. Fools brand people as enemies without understanding the consequences. Unwise 'enemies' cause undesirable consequences. The Master Strategist has wise enemies and so increases his chances of achieving a desirable outcome.

7 RULING

The fundamental questions to contemplate include:

- *How can one be effective at ruling or leading others?*
- *What separates a benevolent leader from an effective one?*
- *Why do leaders fail?*

1   Choice is a function of power. The powerful have it, and may or may not give it to those who lack power.

2   The environment determines what type of people rise to power.

3   The people get what they deserve or are prepared to tolerate what they are not prepared to die for.

4   Rulers are products of history, culture, values, circumstances and, in particular, their subjects.

5   Enlightened rulers are only fit to rule a society that is fit for enlightenment. Similarly, despots are only fit to rule societies that are fit for despotism.

6   Rulers fail when they focus on governing, which is the system or bureaucracy of ruling rather than the object of ruling. Such rulers are embroiled in the system, not the people. The role of the ruler is to unlock human potential. This requires rulers to create the conditions in which people can realise their potential.

7   People are transformed through their senses and behaviours, or through their beliefs, their minds. So, the task of rulers is to change behaviours or to change beliefs. Both are, of course, intertwined.

8   Experiences give rise to feelings, which in turn generate beliefs, which in turn generate behaviour. Changing beliefs can change behaviour. Also, changing behaviour can change beliefs.

9   To pursue the realisation of people's potential, the prerequisites are peace, prosperity and freedom. To realise one's potential, the prerequisites are also war, poverty and oppression. Herein lies the dilemma. Without challenges one does not develop. Extreme challenges are required for development to the furthest boundaries. When challenges become overwhelming, one does not develop. Hence, development is a matter of balance.

10   Hence, oppressors prepare the way for peace, and peace-makers prepare the way for oppressors. The natural cycle involves both.

11   Escape from the cycle begins with taking a view. View leads to choice. Choice comes from power. Power over oneself removes conflict. Hence, view, choice and power are the ingredients for escaping the cycle of freedom–oppression.

12   Only the enlightened escape the cycle of freedom–oppression. Only the enlightened leader can help others escape. Unenlightened leaders can merely fine tune the system of government.

13   Leaders that do good, mostly do accidental good. Accidental because they remain unaware of themselves and of the consequences of their actions. This is the current state of Man; it applies no less to leaders. Intentional good requires a greater level of consciousness, such that their state of being leads to the right outcomes.

14   The lesson for leaders is that they must pursue peace, prosperity and freedom. Peace is learned. Prosperity must be earned. Freedom must be (re)instilled because we lose it over the course of our lives.

8 RESULTS

The fundamental questions to contemplate include:

*   *What is the role of execution in strategy?*
*   *What are the prerequisites for achieving results?*
*   *How frequently does one need to strategise?*

1   The limitations of strategy are imagination, assets and energy. So, unlock the imagination, acquire the assets and add the energy.

2   Pacifism and rigidity in the face of change lead to a lack of fitness to survive.

3   The nature of existence is to engage. This engagement can be conscious or subconscious, constructive or destructive, pre-emptive or reactive. Only death allows us to disengage from the world.

4   Strategies are executed through engagement in the activity of investing and exploiting assets.

5   For execution, strategies are translated into investments; strategists become investors in assets. These assets can be intangible ones, such as time, intellectual ones, such as ideas, and physical ones, such as land, people and machines.

6   Since all such assets are born of the minds of people, investors are essentially investing in minds.

7   Strategists fail when they fail to form an appropriate view, fail to take appropriate positions and fail to exercise appropriate influence.

8   The prerequisite for investing is point of view. The quality of this view is measured by its height, depth and breadth relative to others – its differentiation. The view must change as the situation changes. It must be alive to remain relevant.

9   For execution of strategies, successful strategists take positions that have the characteristics of surviving organisms. Their positions are alive and fit for the situation. Such positions are naturally inclined to be whatever it takes to survive.

10   The superior strategist is not passive, but instead influences the situation – the environment itself. This influence is based on view and position, both of which must be fit to be relevant.

11   The strength of the circle of view, position and influence determine the strength of the investment and its result.

12   Hence, the complete model incorporates view, position and influence.

9 MASTERY

The fundamental questions to contemplate include:

* *What is the personal requirement in mastering strategy?*
* *Why do successful strategists fail?*
* *How does one maximise one's chance of developing into a Master Strategist?*

The Natural Path

1 There is a rhythm to the play. We do not hear the beat. We do not discern the rhythm. We cannot dance in line with the tune. We hear fragments. We feel out of sync. We drown the fragments with noise. This noise appears to be the play. When we have mastery, however, we will be in sync with the rhythm of things and so will flow naturally with that rhythm.

2 The Master Strategist is one who makes himself fit not just for the current environment but also probable environments. Such a person creates the toughest of environments to refine himself and is able to stand above his own personal fear and greed to pursue the most superior outcome that 'fits'.

3 There is a path that is a deeply felt path. This is the path that leads to success. All other paths are contrived.

4 You cannot find your deeply felt path unless you can feel deeply into yourself and into the world.

5 We fail when we follow procedure blindly, closing down sensitivity, awareness and observation.

6 You cannot sustain advantages.

7 To survive, you must focus on being fit for purpose. To

do this you must learn about the environment and attune yourself to it.

8   To prosper, you must flow with the 'natural' order of things; seek balance in your relationships with yourself, others, all things.

Strategy, Environment and Culture

9   The Master Strategist is a master of the environment. Many forms survive. Some live to eat, others to be eaten. The fit survive, but the fittest master their environment. Their mastery is not unnatural, it does not involve a wanton or greedy presence.

10   The tougher the environment, the tougher will be those that survive and those that prosper.

11   In a world with multiple complex environments in which to play, those that emerge as the survivors and prosperous come from the toughest environments.

12   Mastery of one thing leads to mastery of all things. One can learn strategy by doing anything in a powerful, purposeful and principled way. Once learnt, it can be applied to anything.

13   Generalisations help us to understand the general. Encounters are specific. Strategies must be specific.

14   In general, the protégé of a tough environment will beat that of a weaker one. In a specific encounter, however, this should not be assumed to be true. The opponent may have created a tougher environment for himself.

15   The Master Strategist is one who has prospered in the harshest of environments and imposed upon himself the toughest of regimes.

16   To judge who will win, judge who has the best 'system' of testing and developing people.

17   A cell of inhabitants fit to survive, and ruthlessly focused on and capable of winning in the situations they face, can substitute for strategy. The norms of such a cell are what we call 'culture'. Culture can beat strategy if the people of that culture have been honed in an environment that is sharper, tougher and more flexible than that of the strategist's environment. Hence, culture can prevail over strategy.

18   Strategy prevails over culture when there is a major change in the situation or environment that requires a new approach.

19   Great breakthroughs follow maximum oppression. Breakthroughs will come from those who create revolutions. These revolutionaries come from all walks of life: commerce, arts, sciences and military. The cost of their breakthroughs will be high because they are achieved on the foundation of oppression. These revolutionaries will feel that the regimes they live under are oppressive and need to be overturned.

20   In Man's history, oppression has often been institutionalised by personal power-wielders.

21   The cycle of oppression and breakthrough is a feature of Man's development.

22   Oppression is measured by the harshness of the environment. We often call it unjust.

Developing Mastery

23   Self-imposed harshness can be a substitute for environment-imposed or institution-imposed harshness.

24   So, to become a master, self-impose the harshness that will breed mastery. Such is the way of the Master Strategist.

25   Strategists are produced by overcoming barriers. The level at which they play is determined by opportunity. Opportunity may arise or can be created by oneself or by institutions. To maximise the chance of transforming talent into mastery, opportunity must be institutionalised. Every hurdle must be put in the way of this talent to enable testing, elimination and refinement. This will develop instincts. Instinctive actions are faster than thought-out ones. Developing the right instincts is difficult.

26   Do not be narrow in the scope of your definitions of barriers. A tough environment does not merely present physical barriers. The most important tests include emotional, intellectual and intuitive ones.

27   Fear and greed are the roots of most behaviour and so are the roots of most strategies.

28   To understand strategy we must understand fear and greed. The path of fear leads to anger and then to hatred. The path of greed leads to lust and then to malice.

29   We fail because we address hatred. We fail because we address anger. We fail because we fail to address fear. When we find hatred, we must seek anger. When we find anger we must seek fear. Fear is one of the roots.

30   We fail because we address malice. We fail because we address lust. We fail because we fail to address greed. When we find malice, we must seek lust. When we find lust we must seek greed. Lust is the other root.

31   Learning can provide understanding. Meditating can lead to awareness. Action can lead to transformation.

32   The strategy for mastering others is the same as the strategy for mastering one's self.

33   Once you master yourself, there is no need to master anything else. Everything will be as it is meant to be.

THE THREE LAWS OF THE MASTER STRATEGIST

It is in Man's nature to dream and aspire, and then to endeavour, deceive and fight to achieve his dreams and aspirations. Strategy is merely the word we give to the thought that goes into determining how we will prevail. Our ego leads us to believe we should prevail. Our limited view leads us to believe that we understand the consequences of our actions. Our lack of discipline leads us to seek shallow and short-term solutions to complex problems. These facts will not change because they are fundamental constituents of the human condition. However, strategies can be formulated that maximise the chance of delivering 'good'. The strategists formulating such strategies will need to follow three fundamental principles, namely:

1 The Master Strategist must rise above the conflicting bodies and identify a higher common position.
2 The Master Strategist must determine how to take whole and thereby minimise waste and destruction.
3 The Master Strategist must see an event as belonging within a flow of events and so must react within the context of the flow not just the event.

The Master Strategist is capable of rising above the perceived rights and wrongs of a situation to identify a higher, superior position to which both parties could potentially give allegiance. The Master Strategist determines how to 'take whole', that is, without destruction. The Master Strategist does not overreact to individual events, but realises that such events must be seen in the context of a flow of events of past and potential future events.

In the next chapter, we will examine how these principles

can be applied to exercise powerful, purposeful and principled strategy. We will then examine the breakthroughs that are required to overcome the limitations of the prevailing approaches to strategy. In the final chapter, we will consider the subject of Mastery and what it takes to achieve it.

EXERCISING POWER, PURPOSE AND PRINCIPLE

'The Enlightened Strategist is one who can create and combine superior power, purpose and principle. He has superior power such that others accept that he can win so he has no need to exercise power. He has superior purpose such that others accept his purpose. He has the principles that lead others to accept his authority.'

The Book of Power, Purpose and Principle

THE GREAT STRATEGISTS OF THE PAST

In previous eras, the title of strategist was given sparingly. Those who earned it came from many walks of life and had their roots in many disciplines. The examples we most often hail, however, are military leaders, because their results are more self-evident.

Generals These strategists were able to move their armies and those of their enemies to achieve victory. It was understood that, when two armies faced each other, there were many on the field of battle but probably only two Master Strategists and a small handful of companion strategists. Such Master Strategists were often brutal conquerors, such as Genghis

Khan, or idealist Imperialists, such as Alexander the Great and Napoleon.

Philosopher Warriors In the win–lose battles that these strategists fought, they came to question the essence of winning and losing. They ultimately came to understand that their victory was as much over themselves as it was over their enemy and that, ultimately, victory only came if both were achieved. Such men were often warriors such as Miyamoto Musashi, the 17th-century Japanese swordsman, and O Sensei Morihei Ueshiba, the 20th-century Japanese founder of the martial art aikido, which translates as the Way of Harmony.

Socio-Political Intellectuals These were the armchair strategists who threw light on the questions of the acquisition and exercise of games of power. Machiavelli and Clausewitz are men of excellence in this class.

Great Teachers These were the men that revealed the Great Path to Mankind. Their strategies were ones that involved following a path either to enlightenment or to the Heavenly Kingdom. The Buddha and Lao-tzu were ones who revealed such paths.

Mystics Such strategists saw the essence of things and revealed insights to conquer oneself. Often, they were controversial figures, cast as heretics and criminals, and include the 13th-century Christian mystic preacher Meister Eckhart and the 20th-century Indian guru Osho.

The great strategists certainly had information and conducted analysis. The Generals had spies and field agents. The Philosopher Warriors developed a swift ability, almost at an instinctive level, to analyse, position and reposition. The

Socio-Political Intellectuals analysed society, politics and war. The Great Teachers followed a path of self-analysis, meditation and reflection. The Mystics advocated self-experimentation and the experiential way.

The approach of the great strategists enabled them to make leaps and, as a result, their best strategies leapt beyond the conventions of their time. Alexander once raised the land to lower a fort so that he would not have to wage a traditional siege upon it. The O Sensei, Ueshiba, taught that when you find yourself standing in front of the enemy, instead of following the norm of attacking force with force or merely moving aside, you must manoeuvre yourself so that you are standing behind him.

Machiavelli spoke not only of the art of warfare in the traditional sense of forces, manoeuvres and tactics, but of the systematic killing of all those who oppose you, including their relatives, to ensure no future opposition. The Buddha advocated a path beyond only faith and logic when he taught a system for self-realisation that required seekers to accept no doctrine and instead taught methods that helped the seeker to embark on an inward journey. The path led to awareness of the body, the emotions, the mind and the objects of the mind through stillness and observation of its states. Ultimately this method delivers enlightenment. Osho saw Man as a glorious system that could be connected to the whole of creation using its component parts – the body's senses and organs, the brain, the super-conscious mind – and devised strategies that enabled a de- and re-programming of the Man-machine.

Their strategies were more revelation than analysis, more dream than reality, more multi-dimensional than trend projection and more holistic than narrow in scope.

So, given the complexities of our world, what is the model that we need to formulate strategy today?

FORMULATING SUCCESSFUL STRATEGIES

The Three Laws of the Master Strategist – rising above, taking whole and acting with the flow – point to the need to create superior strategists with some notion of 'good' at their core. However, all successful strategies must meet their objectives. There are some prerequisites for formulating successful strategy:

- Look beneath the surface to question the world view.
- Match players to the required attributes and roles.
- Build a strong foundation for your strategy formulation.

Prerequisite One: Look Beneath the Surface

FROM FLAWED WORLD VIEW TO LOOKING BENEATH THE SURFACE

To formulate effective strategy, we need to challenge the simplistic assumptions that we make about the world. We must look a little deeper at the construct of our reality. Most players:

Play by the Rules Most players behave in the context of a construct absorbed from childhood, education, the media, their peers and bosses, and what their society tells them is okay and what is not. These assumed rules are the levers that others use to win. To maintain a code of behaviour in a 'civilised' society, we of course shun the abnormal methods by setting up norms and rules of conduct. The assumptions that their enemy made about what was the 'proper' way to fight was one of the factors that enabled Arjuna and Krishna to succeed in the great Indian epic war between good and evil described in the *Mahabharata*.

Hold Fixed and Simplistic Views of Cause-and-Effect The limits of our education systems enforce simple linear equations upon our minds. We therefore hold simple views of the possibilities. Our training leads us believe 'under circumstance x, y will happen'. This simple equation is formed from past experience and leads us to superimpose the past on our present decisions and to make assumptions about the future effect of our actions. One view regarding the Iraq War of 2003 held that, once the US had won, Iraqis would succumb. The US would then be free to reconstruct Iraq's land and institutions and Iraqis would live by the new rules set. The experience of the Second World War was taken to illustrate the validity of such a view. However, the variables present in the Iraq War included the overwhelming use of technology and information that enabled the war to be concluded in weeks rather than the years taken to defeat the Germans and Japanese. As a result, the Iraqis, unlike their historic predecessors, were not exhausted and did not feel utterly defeated. On the other side, the US did not have re-builders of the type that they had at the end of the Second World War. The conditions for the effect sought were not present.

Limit the Variables Present in any Situation The chance to consider the complexity of any given situation is often eliminated before the strategising begins, because we identify too few variables that could be at work in any situation. In analysing a portfolio of businesses, we consider two things: growth and share. In a more sophisticated analysis of the portfolio, we consider three: growth, share and size. In marketing, we consider four: product, price, place and packaging. In analysing industry structures, we consider five: barriers to entry, product substitution, the relative power of buyers, the relative power of suppliers and rivalry between competitors. And so it goes on. All of these are merely frameworks and guides – which is how some of the inventors intended us to use their frameworks. However, the frameworks that were made for an age when there were less data and less information still drive much of the thinking today. As a result, we continue to ignore variables that are more difficult to quantify, such as the aspirations of our people, the ego of our rival or the fear of failure that drives our own decision-making.

The combination of our conditioning (which leads us to play by the rules), our training (which leads us to consider cause-and-effect in a very simplistic manner) and our limitations (which lead us to consider too few variables) result in a world view that is far too limited, simplistic and predictable. The strategies that result are the same: they are 'normal'. Things seem to run to a pattern that we recognise as 'normal'. In addition, we wish to believe that everything is normal. This allows us to subdue the fear that things may be out of (our) control.

However, things are not as they seem. It is only the 'surface' that moves to a 'normal' pattern. This creates an illusion. The simple equations underlying cause-and-effect that govern our existence mostly hold true and this reinforces the illusion. The reality, however, is that the simple equations are too simple. We need to look beneath the surface to understand the potential outcomes. This look beneath the surface reveals that our simplistic world construct leads us to believe in predictable paths. In fact, the variables that are present in any situation, combined with the variables that are always present in our world context, of the type described earlier as the Seven Shaping Phenomena, are such that an infinite variety of outcomes is possible. As a result, the possible outcome can be chaotic in nature.

So what is the right approach to strategy in a world where anything is possible?

FROM SIMPLISTIC CAUSE AND EFFECT TO CHAOS, PATTERN, INTERCONNECTEDNESS AND CHOICE

To create effective strategies, we must have a broad and sufficiently deep understanding of the world. The quest to understand the world is as old as the history of knowledge. Two approaches, apparently at different ends of the spectrum, sought a Grand Unified Theory of the world: the Buddha felt that this understanding of unification came from one's own consciousness; Einstein felt it lay in the realm of physics. The need to see the patterns underlying apparently random events is an important part of the discipline of strategists. A number of concepts must be added to the thinking of strategists to enable this more 'whole' view to be taken.

The first concept to add to our thinking is that of chaos in relation to cause-and-effect. The first implication of chaos is that, given the vast number of potential variables, there are an infinite number of outcomes and these can be of infinite magnitude. The second thing to bear in mind, is that there is no such thing as an outcome in absolute terms. Or, to look at it differently, there are an infinite number of possible outcomes in a flow of chaotic occurrences. Therefore, the 'outcome' is merely one snapshot. The third thing to bear in mind is that what appears to be chaotic at one level has a pattern if you are able to step back. When you lie on the beach with your head upon the sand and look at the waves there is no discernible pattern to their form. This is true. However, when you walk up the cliff and look down on the beach, you can clearly see the pattern of the waves in their ebb and flow. This is also true. The pattern may lead us to reach immediately for a conclusion about waves in all circumstances. This is the trap of the popularised framework.

Man's study of the universe is beginning to reveal patterns. The study of the cosmos is beginning to reveal the pattern of the flow of the universe. The study of the solar system is beginning to reveal the pattern of the flow of the forces between, and on, planets. The study of our planet is beginning to reveal the pattern of the flow of life on our planet. The study of the body and mind is beginning to reveal the pattern of a human being's existence. So, our strategies will need to discern the patterns in what appears to be chaos.[1]

The second concept to add to our thinking is that of interconnectedness. All outcomes are snapshots and, as we have just seen, they are the consequence of the interaction of infinite variables. Let us look at each outcome as a thing. This thing can be tangible, a product created, or intangible, an emotion. Each thing is a consequence of the interaction of other things. By interaction, we mean the cause-and-effect relationship. So, the existence of each thing is dependent on another thing. At the most simple level, we can say they are co-existent and interdependent and our strategies will need to recognise this inherent interdependence of all things. The implication is that our strategies are not, as we often see them, ends in themselves, but are laden with consequence.

We have one more concept to add to our thinking. This is the notion of 'contextual choice', that is, at the individual level, choice takes place within a specific mindset, a context, that determines how we approach strategy. The optimistic view will hold that, 'if anything is possible, we have the potential to make anything happen'. The pessimistic view will hold that, 'if anything is possible, we have the potential to make nothing happen'. The impotent mind will say that 'almost nothing is in my control'. The megalomaniac mind will say that 'everything is in my control'. Is it as simple as that? Is it just about the mind-set? The answer is that if we begin with the mind, it is as simple as that. Our strategy is about the interventions we wish to make, based on the world view we hold. If we start at another extreme, the universe, our strategy is formed in the context of the greater pattern. So our choices will need to be made based on a view of the situation.

Choice is a function of power. The powerful are powerful because they can choose whether or not to share their power with others. They are also powerful because we let them make that choice. So power is gained or lost based on the choices that we make and are allowed to make. Events or outcomes arise either from deliberate choices or 'random' or chaotic interactions, ones that we cannot see as a direct result of our choices. Chaos is both the result of deliberate choices and random interactions. So, whatever strategy we adopt, it ultimately leads to a transitory outcome within a broader flow of events.

FROM STRATEGY AS EVENT TO STRATEGY AS FLOW

In the field of physics and quantum mechanics, the physicist David Bohm argued for a holistic view of the universe. He felt that we would need to learn to regard matter and life as a whole, as a coherent domain.[2] The 'softer' and swifter Chinese martial arts, such as Wing Chun, require the practitioner to flow smoothly and quickly from one position to the next in the face of an assault from many unpredictable forces. The 'harder' traditions are said to be based more on the use of strength, and are therefore more rigid, which in turn restricts their ability to respond to change. Strategists have much to learn from the concept of strategy as a 'flow of actions'.

The temptation is to see strategy as a one-off event. Strategy is too often conducted as a calendarised activity – as is budgeting, accounting or inventory taking – whereas, in reality, it consists of action and reaction to the world. The world does not begin and end and neither does strategy. The forces of change are constantly biting at us. Sometimes they bite at the edges of our body, and so we do not feel them, sometimes deep within the body, and so again we do not feel them, and sometimes in multiple places, so we do not see the pattern of their attack. The gross nature of our awareness fails us. We become insensitive to the forces at play. Strategy needs to be sensitive to the forces at work so that it can be constantly applied to these forces. The flow of change needs to be matched by a strategy that also flows.

The basics of formulating strategy will need to change so that we:

- Become sensitive to a broader set of variables.
- Think of the flow of events and the outcome as a mere snapshot in that flow.
- Seek the pattern in the chaotic flow.
- Seek to understand the interconnectedness of all things.
- Examine the consequences of our actions.

Adopting this approach will make our world view more mature, make us more sensitive to change and more adaptive to the forces around us. The conscious requirement for the strategist is to:

- Exercise choice in the context of the awareness of the 'natural' flow of change, and
- Take the ego out of the strategy, since whatever we achieve is not entirely a product of us.

These things are not possible for those who have not achieved a state of enlightenment. We, the unenlightened, will fail to be sufficiently aware and sufficiently egoless. We can but try. The product of such an approach to strategy is 'Mature Strategy'.

Prerequisite Two: Match Players to Required Attributes and Roles

The existence of 'Mature Strategy' is dependent on the maturity of the strategist and the maturity of his world view. The distinction is, of course, artificial, but is made here to illustrate two requirements: the development of personal attributes and the development of understanding.

As stated earlier, in situations requiring strategy, there is usually one strategist and many operatives. Although many of the operatives have names that sound as if they are strategists, their experience has only prepared them to be operatives. Some operatives will be better experienced at dealing with situations than others. Amongst them there will be those with power or influence and therefore the ability to make their views prevail. This presents an opportunity to defeat the opponent (if defeating is your game). The culture, process, relationships and weaknesses of your opponent may prevent them from being clear about who is and who is not the strategist. Therefore, understanding the culture and strategy-formulating process of your opponents is a key aspect of strategic positioning (if positioning is your game).

Most strategy-formulation processes involve a collective decision-making formula. The collective steps are carried out through activities such as 'brainstorming', which are often carried out to solve problems, prioritise activities, set objectives and targets. Brainstorming is usually, but not always, an indication that there is a lack of leadership regarding strategy in the room. It is critical not to confuse strategy formulation with the need for communication and 'buy in'.

When facing an opponent who uses a brainstorming technique, look for one of four situations:

Situation One: The Master and Novices This consists of brainstorming amongst a Master Strategist and a group of significantly less mature strategists. Apart from accidents, this will lead to an inferior strategy to the one that can be developed by the Mature Strategist alone, unless the Mature Strategist is prepared to manipulate the situation to secure his desired outcome.

Situation Two: The Master and Apprentices of Mixed Maturity Brainstorming amongst a Master and those spread along the maturity spectrum can lead to marginal improvements upon the strategy of the Mature Strategist alone. Improvements will result from the ability of others, particularly specialists and those closer in maturity to the Master Strategist, to highlight other factors for the consideration of the Master Strategist. Their contribution is one of information rather than strategy.

Situation Three: A Group of Masters Brainstorming amongst a peer group of Mature Strategists can lead to a higher quality strategy because of the different, but equally high quality, insights. This possesses the characteristic of a council of strategists rather than a brainstorming session.

Situation Four: Enlightened Strategist. Brainstorming with someone at the 'ultimate' level is unnecessary. The result cannot be improved.

The extent of the improvement in the strategy formulated by the strategist depends on the maturity of the participants, the process itself and the data used. Where the strategy of our opposite number is based on situations one or two, in other words a flawed process, we have more chance of success.

Good strategy formulation requires honesty and clarity about the roles involved. The other roles fall into two categories: roles primarily focused on providing the inputs to the strategist and roles focused on the execution of the strategy.

The input roles are covered by data and information gatherers who will collect the data and information required to enable the strategist to get to work; analysts who will analyse this data and information to help the strategist understand the nature of it; and technical specialists who will determine the details of the methods that can be used to implement the strategies.

The execution roles are covered by leaders with the responsibility for action. These leaders will fall into various formations and hierarchies and will be organised to cover all aspects of the execution of the strategy.

In both the input and execution roles there will be those that aspire to become strategists. Through experience they can develop their maturity, refine themselves and develop a strategic outlook. The assimilation of these experiences into strategic capability, however, is a rarity. Few have the determination to undergo the rigours of self-mastery required to develop maturity. The conditions for this assimilation are unique to each individual, but there are some lessons we can draw and we will do so in Chapter six.

In conclusion, there are many analysts and executors but few strategists. It is critical to be honest in the definition of roles.

Prerequisite Three: Build a Strong Foundation for your Strategy Formulation

The gathering of data has long been understood as a prerequisite for strategy formulation. In the ancient world, Sun Tzu of China, Chanakya of India and the ninja of Japan all recognised the critical importance of data and information, just as the CIA does today.

The foundations of good strategy have been undermined by

a number of factors, which have been discussed in this work. One of the further factors undermining the foundations of good strategy arises from the idealisation of too many of our modern leaders as heroes. This has led to the concentration of power and resulted in a pressure to act. Those leaders with a bias towards action appear decisive and have more chance of retaining their leadership. Those with a bias towards action seek positions that require action. The bias towards action of leaders in high profile situations leads to the most fundamental errors in achieving strategic objectives, because the foundations of their strategies are weak. When action is built on a solid foundation it has the maximum chance of delivering results.

Is it not possible to move straight to results? Certainly a culture built for success can do this, but only until a major change occurs in the environment that is beyond the experience of the culture. At that point strategy is required. Unfortunately, a great many seek to get straight to results too quickly. The reasons for this are:

Too Many 'Macho Leaders' Act Before Thinking They fail to consider the relevant facts and the consequences.

Too Many 'Analysts' Stop at Analysis They fail to take into account and use the experience, intuition, wisdom, strategic minds and action of others.

Too Many of the 'Older Generation' Stop at Experience and Intuition They fail to absorb new data, information and knowledge. Their assumptions about the validity of their world view, based on their legacy, also stops them from moving towards wisdom.

Too Many 'Religious Leaders and Gurus' Stop at Wisdom They fail to apply their wisdom to the problems of the world and so fail to do their utmost to act in the interests of other sentient beings. Their fascination lies with their own energies, mind and consciousness. They leave the fate of the world to those less wise.

The results of such 'strategists', who are driven too much by the bias towards action, do not benefit from fully going through the cycle of analysis, experience and intuition, wisdom, strategy and, finally, action.

The other variables to consider in strategy formulation are time and context. One can consider everything possible, and so be too slow given the changes in the environment or the changes in the context.

There are a few things, in particular, to bear in mind in strategy formulation. The first, and most important, is that strategy is about achieving an outcome, a result. The second is that, to achieve this outcome, a number of conditions or states are required and that 'result' is one of the states of strategy. The final thing to say is that 'interventions', or actions, are required to make progress towards the achievement of the result.

The function of strategy is to deliver a result. Result is one of Five States, which become apparent because of Four Interventions:

1   The Founding State is Data and Information.
2   With the intervention of Analysis, Data and Information is transformed into the State of Knowledge.
3   With the intervention of Experience, Knowledge is transformed into the State of Insight.
4   With the intervention of Wisdom, Insight is transformed into the State of Foresight
5   With the intervention of Strategy and Action, Foresight is transformed into Results.

EXERCISING POWER, PURPOSE, PRINCIPLE

Power

In popular culture, power is generally evidenced by fighting and winning. The battle for superior power focuses on competition, disruption and domination. The greatest power is the ability to win without having to fight.

COMPETITION

A successful Strategy of Competition results in a defeated rival. Rivals are most effectively defeated when their mind is defeated. The other option is to destroy their people and assets. A strategy of destruction requires the destroyer to abandon the hope of taking world opinion and support with them. It is a path that is, and will continue to be, increasingly difficult to justify in a world of open distribution of, and open access to, news events. Strategies of competition are based on shifting the balance of power in our favour.

Three of the key reasons for strategies of competition are:

Limited Resources The argument is that there are limited resources and so we must fight for our share of them. At any point in time this is true about the basic resources with which we can achieve our ambitions. This path leads to a long cycle of building resources and then destroying each others' resources

Limited Opportunity The argument is that the number of good opportunities is scarce and so we must fight for our share of those that arise. This is true of any opportunity that we choose to compete for. In other words, the argument is a circular one. This path is based on the assumption that we must rely on opportunities arising, as opposed to creating them, and is implicity based on a belief that imagination and creativity are limited. This path leads to many players pursuing a large volume of similar ideas in the hope that they will somehow outmanoeuvre others

Limited Time The argument is that we have limited time to achieve our ambitions. Again, for any specific period, the argument holds true since we are constrained by the time allocated by company research analysts to deliver a return (one quarter), by investors and shareholders to deliver results (one year), by electorates to deliver on our promises (four years). This path leads us to place an artificial constraint on our strategies, but it is a real constraint if you play by the rules of others.

At any point in time, these constraints are valid. However, these temporary constraints have become limiting factors, constants, assumptions and common wisdom. There is a more fundamental truth: these three limitations are self-imposed constraints and delusions. They enable us to ignore the deeper reality which is that we pursue strategies of competition because we are not smart enough to do things that enable us to avoid competing. Even more fundamentally, the real rationale for the pursuit of strategies of competition has its basis in human failings. The key failings arise from assumptions and beliefs, which include the following:

- The belief that beating others is natural.
- The assumption that people perform best when they are afraid.
- The belief that aggression is a requirement for getting one's way.
- The belief that the ends justify the means.

- The belief that there is always a price to be paid and it should be the other person that pays.
- The belief that it is right to use might.

Such beliefs and assumptions lead to the use of might, the exploitation of people and the waste of resources. Such strategies lead to the principles of war, which are then applied to business, and are not the most effective way of creating value.

The most effective strategies are based on conquering the mind. Modern strategic method fails us by failing to prepare us for this battle. Legacies, resources and capital are not the basis of competition. Competition is essentially about a battle for the mind. There are three potential players: you, your enemy and the 'target' of your battle. At a basic level, to beat the mind of an opponent requires the undermining or corrupting of the opponent's mind and the winning of the target's mind. The opponent can be said to be corrupted when he is no longer flexible; no longer fit to survive. The methods for winning the mind include the following:

Stalling your Opponent's Ability to Take the Initiative This requires you to cause your rival to avoid change so that the initiative is lost. The Japanese consumer electronics industry had so strongly accepted the supremacy of the Japanese market during the 1980s and 1990s that they missed the personal computing wave, the internet wave and the global mobile wave. The rest of the world pioneered and profited because of the failure of the Japanese, rather than because they had outwitted them. Master Strategists would be capable of engineering such outcomes.

Forcing Emotional Responses This requires you to induce your rival to suppress their natural response so that emotional responses prevail. In the first few years of the 21st century, during the second Iraq War, the release of photographs of American soldiers torturing Iraqi prisoners elicited outrage in America and divided the country. The American President faced the prospect of winning the war, but losing the Presidency. Master Strategists would be capable of engineering such outcomes.

Causing their Judgement to be Questioned This requires you to make your rival give inadequate consideration to the facts of the situation, resulting in shallow judgement. In the 1930s, Hitler was able to build his forces and positions in Europe without intervention because the European nations were too willing to believe that a war could be avoided. They failed to respond to, what now appears to be, the clear intent underlying Hitler's campaign. Master Strategists would be capable of engineering such outcomes.

Causing Internal Dissension in your Rivals This requires you to bring about a breakdown of trust within the opponent's organisation. The UN failed to unite in the second American-led campaign in Iraq in the early years of the 21st century. The dictator, Saddam Hussein, was able to offer enough access to his country to convince many of America's allies of his intention to disarm. As a result, the American-led invasion of Iraq was derided by the French and Germans, in particular, and declared to be illegal by the Secretary-General of the United Nations. Master Strategists would be capable of engineering such an outcome.

Causing them to Rely on their Legacy This requires you to induce formulaic and pragmatic responses and the subsequent suppression of your opponent's imagination. Alexander was able to rely on the 'meet force with force' approach of the Persian army: the Barbarian hordes were able to rely on the known battle tactics of the Roman army; after the independence of Southern Ireland from the British

Empire, India was able to benefit from the limited appetite of the British to use brutality to retain their Indian empire. Master Strategists would be capable of engineering such outcomes.

Enemies are beaten when their assumptions, beliefs and values are undermined. However, competition leads to retaliation. This is a natural result of the principle of cause-and-effect. So, finally, it is important to remember that the battle for the mind can take many other more positive forms when the mind is won over, rather than beaten.

DISRUPTION

A successful Strategy of Disruption causes a change to the course, functioning or nature of the enemy's system. This is akin to infecting the enemy with a virus. For this purpose, the system may be a political system, a system of enterprise and economics, an investment or market system, or a community, family or way of life. Three of the most popular ways of implementing strategies of disruption are:

To Leverage Others The argument is that a small force cannot compete head on with a larger force. So, smaller players, who are usually competitors, band together to attack a common foe. This path has the potential benefit of a magnified force applied to the enemy. The risk is that the smaller forces, who are usually also foes, will fail to act as one.

To Use Limited Force The argument is that it is not always necessary to destroy the enemy. The objective is to make a controlled impact, in essence to have a 'limited war'. This path, if successful, leads to minimal destruction. The concept of a 'limited nuclear war' was much discussed in the 20th

century, with a strong expectation that retaliation would escalate to a full nuclear war. The nature of such a technique is often such that once a disruption is launched it is difficult to control, particularly when two large foes face each other
To Surprise The argument is that protection is better afforded and objectives are more likely to be achieved with covert action. The objective is to strike where it is not expected. If successful, this path leads to confusion in the mind of the enemy, who, as a result, will have difficulty in responding.

Strategies of disruption are also destructive, but have other noteworthy characteristics which provide options for strategists, including using a single attacker or multiple attacker; taking an overt or covert approach; and determining the extent of damage to be inflicted. In particular, when fighting an overwhelmingly large force, direct attack is futile. Instead disruption is required. Disruptions can be one-off major events that shake the system or they can be small shocks that cumulatively undermine the system. Innovation is required to create disruptions. Disruptions can be 'bred'. The methods for creating disruption include the following:

Breeding Enmity so that the new generation hate or disrespect the enemies of the older generation. Such tactics preserve age-old rivalries and prevent successive generations creating peace, as we saw in the 20th century and the early 21st century in Israel and Palestine, Northern Ireland and Britain, Islam and the US, India and Pakistan.
Breeding Independent Attack Units each of which is incentivised to act to a predetermined pattern. Such units can be the 'sleepers' of the Cold War or the thousands of entrepreneurial game developers of Sony, each of whom was

incentivised to attack the business rivals of Sony in the video games industry.

Breeding New Technology that creates new behaviours in order to attack the prevailing way of doing things. Such technologies included the DVD home film format, which attacked the existence of cinemas, the peer-to-peer file swapping systems that led to consumption without payment and thereby undermined the music industry, the mobile camera phone images of brutality against prisoners in Iraq in the second Iraq War that, passed around on the internet, undermined the US effort to establish its credibility in Iraq.

Such disruptions can behave like viruses by attacking and undermining the performance of the target. Modern strategic theory has not yet adapted to the fact that there is now a network that interconnects individual entities. These networked entities behave as if they were a live system. The mode of most modern strategy is to focus on the individual entities. As a result, the strategy approach is inadequate for dealing with more complex systems such as the internet and Asian extended business communities (such as the Keiretsu) and terrorists. By their very nature such strategies require a more in-depth understanding of the nature of the enemy and his reaction; the network or system within which the disruption will act; and the carriers of the virus, which can be an idea or concept, a human being or a technology. Viral strategies are a core part of such network-system-based contexts. In creating a virus-based strategy the following principles are critical to success:

Secrecy and Spread The most effective virus will spread quickly and be difficult to track to its origin.

Adaptive Gene The intelligent virus will be adaptive to the situation and will learn to survive assault.

Multiple Architectures To disable a large and strong protagonist, many viruses may be required. Each virus must have a different design for maximum effect. In this way, there will be no common defence against the viruses.

Disruptive strategies can be deployed by giants as well as small forces. However, the tendency of the giant is to use overwhelming force as a matter of course. This highly effective method ends up becoming a habit, which then becomes a characteristic or state of operation that stifles creativity, sensitivity and awareness, and leads to vulnerability to attack by disruptive virus strategies. However, the way in which you undermine your opponent's strategies is also the way in which your own strategies can be undermined.

So, finally, it is important to remember that to be successful at such disruptive strategies, and to avoid the retaliation that may come from a larger opponent, the strategist must remain the invisible mastermind behind the scenes. The ego generally prevents this most essential of states.

DOMINATION

A successful Strategy of Domination results in a state of followership amongst rivals. 'Followership' is defined here as a set of characteristics that result in a propensity to let others lead. Domination over rivals comes from the existence of sustained uneven power in relationships. Domination by the few over the many is a natural result of the interaction between living organisms. Countless experiments show how, in any given environment, the growth pattern leads to many competing organisms being replaced by a few who, over time, outlive their fitness to survive and are disrupted and displaced by new, fitter entities. The ego causes leaders to believe that this will not happen to them. For some reason, they believe they will remain immortal leaders of their empires, nations, companies, communities, families and lives. Three key reasons for strategies of domination are:

The Superiority Complex The argument is that the dominant are dominant because they are inherantly superior or have a superior way, product or service. This superiority is argued as a right that entitles them to enforce their way on others. This is similar to the moral justification of destructive strategists. It usually, but not always, is based on the possession of some measurable and demonstrable superiority. This path ignores the transient nature of superiority and the unstable nature of the relationship between the superior and inferior which rests on maintaining a win–lose relationship.

Survival of the Most Efficient Very simply put, the argument is that the consolidation of power in the hands of one, or a few, results in greater efficiency in the utilisation of resources. There is indeed a strong link between scale and efficiency, at least in the medium term. This path has short-term validity, but carries the penalty of delaying the introduction of innovations.

Progress and Common Good The argument is that large monopolistic entities provide the best chance of establishing standards. The US anti-trust authorities have attacked various companies suspected of monopolistic powers, including IBM and Microsoft. Both have been able to establish global standards because of their substantial industry positions. Such standards are said to provide a common level of performance for all, and so are for the common good. Such a path may indeed provide benefits, but again the setting of standards beyond their usefulness is merely a path for ensuring conformity and preventing innovation.

Inevitably, dominance leads to domineering behaviour. The dominant lose their perspective and end up believing in their right to dominate, as if it were 'God-given'. In the 21st century, such a scenario could happen if America were to believe it had a God-given right to police the world, if Microsoft were to believe it had a God-given right to own every operating system and take predatory measures to exclude others, if GE were to believe it had a God-given right to be the winner of every contract bid that it was interested in, and if Big Pharma believed it had a God-given right to control access to life-saving medicines. All of these dominant institutions have delivered enormous value. The question is when do the dominant become domineering? Such changes are subtle; they are about character. Character leads to behaviour. However, behaviour can corrupt character too.

Domination should be tempered by recognition of the role of the dominated. A state of domination exists when the dominated remain fearful and lack self-confidence; there is a lack of innovation; the inability to cause or exploit disruption in the environment prevailed; and the dominated stay weak and fail to develop themselves. Such conditions can of course be created and sustained by a skilful dominant player. Domination does not, however, have to be exploitative in all its phases. To establish domination requires only that one possesses something desirable and that one shares sufficient benefits to create a pattern of followership. The methods for creating domination include the following:

Possession of a One-Off Advantage of Sufficient Scale to create significant distance between the holder and others. The Roman army's use of weapons and methods, such as the famous tortoise formation of shields, created a one-off advantage of sufficient scale to create significant distance between the less structured methods of 'barbarians' and themselves. Others could not close the gap and the Romans went on to govern an empire comprising more than 40 nations today. IBM's use of government contracts following the end of the Second World War enabled the company to create the biggest data-processing machines in the world, allowing it to create significant distance between itself and others. Others could not close this gap and, by the late 1970s, IBM owned over 60 per cent of the value of the global computing industry.[3]

Possession of a Renewable Advantage and the ability to renew that advantage. The British Empire's ability to understand the nature of peoples all over the world, and to adapt their approach using a combination of trade, force and a political ability to institute policies such as 'divide and rule', enabled them to sustain an empire for over 350 years. At its height, the British Empire occupied over 20 per cent of the world's land area. Similarly, the ability of Nokia to understand how to create fun, empathy and loyalty using a combination of research and development, a few product platforms, global buying power, global distribution, branding and marketing enabled them to reach a global ownership of approximately 35 per cent of the world's mobile phone market in the three years 2000 to 2003.[4]

A Stagnant Environment so that effective competing offerings are not created. The Egyptians ruthlessly preserved an order based on religious, political and sociological rules that enabled a Pharaoh system to last over 3,000 years by, amongst other factors, controlling the pace of change and innovation. The unchallenged interpretation of the Christian faith during the 1000 years of the European Middle Ages meant that it presided over a period with comparatively fewer significant developments in the arts, philosophy, maths and literature than the periods of history just before and afterwards. The Microsoft Operating System maintained about 95 per cent market share in an era with no rival, yet its own system, after two decades, was judged to have managed only to mirror its much smaller rival, Apple.[5] **Targets Willing to be Dominated** because the price of freedom is too high. It is estimated that up to the 20th century, 40 million people were killed in wars and 133 million as a result of genocide. However, in the 20th century alone, nearly 40 million were killed in wars and 170 million died as a result of genocide. The catalyst that causes people in large numbers to rise up and demand change can come from either violence or non-violence. The US secured freedom from the British in 1776 after a violent war of independence, whereas India secured its freedom in 1947 after a war of non-violent protest. Both won in part when the price of sustaining domination was too high.[6]

The aim of the dominant is to sustain their domination. Domination can bestow significant benefits upon the many and enables a new plateau to be reached for the population. Domination beyond its usefulness, however, leads to predatory behaviour because it becomes habitual and steps are to be taken to sustain the power position beyond its 'natural' time. Domination becomes 'unnatural' when it is sustained beyond the point where sufficient advantages are conferred to give up freedom. Only when there is an understanding of balance can domination strategies survive and even then no advantage is sustainable indefinitely. When sustained 'unnaturally', domination leads to rebellion.

In conclusion, a higher purpose is required to guide and temper power-based strategies.

Purpose

In popular culture, purpose is about the fulfilling of personal ambitions. The battle for superior purpose focuses initially on creating a superior cause. The aim is to transform a superior cause into a common cause. Superior causes are established through either deception or shared truth. Establishing a common cause by using deception is perilous but can be successful. Establishing one through a shared truth is more likely to solicit cooperation. The latter requires inclusion: a more open approach that involves confessing one's wrongs, compromising, aspiring together and sharing things we hold dear. Battles of competition, disruption and domination result in winners and losers. No one is immune from retaliation – this is plain cause-and-effect. The most effective strategies avoid such waste of resources.

INCLUSION

A successful Strategy of Inclusion involves collaboration so that the partners can win together. This is possible in many situations and is the core principle underlying global alliances throughout history. Three of the key reasons for strategies of inclusion are:

> ***Synergy Between Assets*** The argument is that two organisations working together with complementary assets can provide better results. This was the rationale for the huge number of mergers of companies in the 1990s. At an operational level, this requires the two to combine their resources in a way that results in a more positive value than any one of the two alone. This path offers a way to combine and create superiority. However, most executors of such strategies fail to eradicate duplicate resources, or to select

the best resources to prevail or to establish the best process for the two organisations to work together.

To Succeed Against a Bigger Rival The argument is that combined forces have more chance of defeating a larger opponent. This strategy can be applied to attack or defence, against a common enemy or not, and to either mitigate risks or to invest. This path offers an opportunity to pursue one of the power strategies. However, it is often pursued by those with common weaknesses combining forces rather than those with complementary strengths. Such coalitions of the weak can result in even weaker positions for all collaborators.

Common Goals The argument is that two entities with common goals can avoid competing, dividing and spoiling if they can work together. In addition such a strategy offers an opportunity to achieve more faster and with less. This path requires the participants to have assessed the common ground and compatibility of their leaders, assets and cultures. In the absence of such attributes, common goals do not deliver superior results.

Unfortunately, many inclusive strategies are the product of fear, weakness, lack of courage, greed or ideology. The rationale for inclusion may be based on an analytic justification, a macho-ego justification or an ideological one. Many analytic justifications, based on a largely numbers-based approach, fail to address the real issues of marrying two entities with different characters and behaviours. The ego-based rationales do use analysis to demonstrate the benefits of the combination, but the analysis masks a decision to proceed regardless of the costs and so ignores the practical risks of failure. The ideological rationales ignore the analysis, the ego and the difficulties and instead act from a notion of right and wrong.

The greater the magnitude of the objective and the greater the complexity of the environment, the greater the requirement for a strategist to magnify the impact of the resources available. Magnification of resources comes from unleashing the power of the individual, the entity and others. Magnification requires inclusion. The more difficult a situation is for one party to handle exclusively, the greater the need for inclusion. However, all inclusion involves the abandonment of initially separate identities in favour of a lesser or greater merger of identities. So inclusion is essentially about the merging or combining of two separate organisms. As such it requires an understanding of the 'DNA' of the organisms to establish whether a combination is feasible. The methods for creating inclusion, or different degrees of inclusion, are as follows:

Agreeing Rules Combining or coordinating to have the power to determine the rules by which others participate.
Aligning Goals Aligning goals so that activities are coordinated and an agreed result is achieved.
Combining Activities or Initiatives Combining activities or initiatives to achieve a cause, a specific event to occur or a performance level to be reached.
Merging Organisations Merging the organisms to gain scale and other economic and competitive advantages or satisfy ego objectives.

The key requirements of the strategist are threefold. Firstly, the strategist must reconcile conflicting aims. The merger boom of the late 20th century was founded on cutting costs, climbing industry league tables, building global empires, gaining competitive advantages and, sometimes, merely following the merger wave. During the same period a number of other strategic initiatives struggled to be totally inclusive:

- the European Union of nations was designed to create a powerful trading bloc to more effectively trade between countries but also to negotiate better with the other national powers and trading blocs. However, it often found itself in internal power struggles and disagreements over issues as fundamental as trade, military policy and governance.
- the international unions such as the United Nations and the IMF sought to create a powerful force for resolving international issues but often found themselves in conflict with US trade and foreign policy.
- military coalitions such as NATO sought to combine the force of nations to provide peace in troubled regions but often struggled to agree the timing and strategy for engagement and found themselves unable to intervene to prevent the mass murders in the Balkans and Rwanda in the 1990s.

Secondly, the strategist must direct, reconcile and redirect people's energy. Inclusive strategies fail because of the inability of the entities involved to move as one and to adapt adequately to changing circumstances. Organisations are expected to behave in certain ways after an act of inclusion, but often continue to act in their previous way. This independent action is contrary to agreement and leads to suspicion. If unchecked, it leads to a breakdown of trust. Such failures, which are the responsibility of the strategist, arise because of the failure to reconcile and to redirect people's energy.

Thirdly, the strategist must develop higher or superior common purpose. Although this is often the critical first step, I have put it last because of the difficulty of achieving this purpose. True inclusive strategies are based on a 'pure' state of mind, pure in the sense that there is an absence of deceit. Deceit comes from the undeclared intention to pursue a strategy of competition, disruption and domination. In such cases, the strategy of inclusion is a cloak.

Only an Enlightened Strategist can pursue inclusion, since no other has a pure mind. A strategy of inclusion is a commitment to the Master Strategist, a goal to the superior strategist and a weapon to the effective strategist. History points to the difficulty of pursuing an inclusive path. Both the Buddha and Christ were able to pursue an inclusive path. The Buddha worked in his lifetime to understand and translate his enlightenment into instruction and techniques for achieving awareness so that others would be included in the prize that he had uncovered. Christ worked in his lifetime to reveal the path to his Father's house. In business, international and military affairs this has proven far more difficult.

In conclusion, truly inclusive strategies require a maturity and selflessness that are difficult for leaders to achieve. Since true inclusion requires the absence of the motive of personal gain we are more likely to find it in religious and spiritual contexts, rather than in military or business ones.

ASPIRATION

A successful Strategy of Aspiration aims to redefine the existing reality. Such a strategy recognises that to redefine the way things are, it is necessary to redefine the beliefs and aspirations of people. It is an approach which begins with aspiration rather than analysis, which is seen as a tool to refine the strategy. Three of the key reasons for strategies of aspiration are:

I Have a Dream . . . The argument is that there is a better way. In 1963, Martin Luther King described a better way where Black Americans and White Americans would live together and raised the aspirations of the American people in his famous address that began with the words, 'I have a dream . . .'. This path has the potential to capture the imagination of people by touching their innermost desires and aspirations. Such a path, in the hands of charismatic leaders who seek competition, disruption or domination, can also lead to destruction. Genghis Khan, Attila the Hun and Adolf Hitler's reportedly charismatic speeches during their campaigns of domination achieved such an effect. Followers therefore need to question the dream and understand the potential consequences.

Stalemate The argument is that the existing situation is deadlocked in a cycle of stagnation or destruction and can only be broken by an aspirational approach.

An example of a spiralling circle of violence is the Israel–Palestine conflict of the late 20th and early 21st centuries. The Palestinians had felt the might and effectiveness of the Israeli Army with its advanced technology and weaponry on a regular basis. The Israelis had felt the terror-capability and effectiveness of a smaller and crudely equipped force of Palestinian suicide bombers and saboteurs who had fought with a determination equal to their opponents'. Both sides had used a strategy of retaliation and pre-emption to kill each other but, in the process, had also destroyed their own way of life. Even after years of pursuing the cycle of violence, both sides had failed repeatedly to find a common aspiration and translate it into actions that would break the stalemate.

In 1990, newly released from prison, the visionary black leader Nelson Mandela called for an end to the attacks on both sides in his country and, in an unlikely alliance with F. W. de Klerk, the white South African President, took the actions that led to the breakdown of the spiral of violence. Such a path requires the complicity of aggressors on both sides. Here principles play a critical role; in situations where there is an entrenched spiral of violence, negotiation is useless without the right principles. Every failure merely deepens the pattern of failure and perpetuates the spiral of violence.

Making a Difference The argument is that to make a difference one has to leap beyond the accepted way and create something new. This something will be aspirational. Neither the experts, the researchers, the analysts nor the financiers will find a rational basis for approving the idea.

In 1979, Sony's introduction of the Walkman mobile music device not only shattered the perception that Japanese products were cheap and inferior, it catapulted the company into the position of technological pace-setter. However, at its inception, Sony's co-founder, Akio Morita, had difficulty convincing his product team even to support its development. The Walkman device was to go on to become the benchmark product of the industry.

In 2003, Apple Computers launched a music device to redefine the mobile music experience by combining hardware, software and content through a digital service. They demonstrated the sharpest thinking of the time by showing Sony customers that form and function must fulfil a fantasy. The beautifully formed iPod music player, with its library of cheap music, elicited an emotional response in users all around the world and made Sony's walkman a contender instead of a leader.

Such paths require the power to execute a vision where the consensus runs contrary to the view of the visionary. The danger is that the visionary takes his followers on an inappropriate path, is not in tune with the situation or the environment and therefore is deluded. Lenin's passionate pursuit of Communism proved, by the end of the 20th century, to be such a path.

Aspirational strategists touch the innermost desires of people through their intuitive ability to grasp the essence of the times, the environment and the situation. Such an ability is a powerful one. And, as such, it carries with it the temptation of pursuing dangerous personal agendas. The essence of aspiration-based strategies is as follows:

Beyond the Past An aspirational approach does not base the strategy on an analysis of yesterday, but instead defines a dream that is worthy of the entity – its people, assets and history – and fit for the environment and situation.

Infinite Paths Aspiration-based strategies recognise the huge diversity of potential paths and assert that there is no need for each of us to follow the same path.

Without Conflict Winning without conflict is an essential aspect of aspirational strategy. This is a matter of avoiding waste. The core belief is that to aim to defeat others is the wrong place to begin.

Higher purpose If you rise to the highest purpose you will be beyond contention and will have the opportunity to reconcile. The higher purpose of the aspiration is to change minds and behaviours and to enhance lives.

The methods for creating aspiration include the following:

Innovation Great innovations have come from pioneers who sought power, fame, wealth or a greater good and, as a result, have changed the human condition. Aspirers have driven enormous innovations, which, in the 20th century, have included the aeroplane, the invention of durable plastic, the theory of relativity, the discovery of penicillin, the transistor, rocket fuel and space flight, the electronic computer, the heart transplant, the test-tube baby, the moon landing, the cellular phone and cloning.

Growth They do not merely compete or rely on the legacy of their assets. Waves of growth have the potential to create momentum around an idea and have driven enormous optimism. These waves are particularly evident in the great 'gold rushes' of antiquity when hundreds of thousands flocked to great cities such as Alexandria to build new civilisations, and later to the booming city of San Francisco to mine gold, as well as, in the 1990s, the virtual city of the internet to build the new technology era.

Expansion and Exploration They seek to go beyond the known territories. Leaders have often driven people to sacrifice themselves to the dream of charting new territories and realising unimagined rewards. The European empires explored Africa, India, Japan and Cathay with the hope of acquiring magical wonders and untold wealth.

Change They are adaptive and stay relevant to the environment. The greatest challenge is to adapt to new circumstances. Great leaders do not attach themselves to the current formula for success. Alexander embraced the ways of the Persians, the Egyptians and the Indians during his campaigns.

Influence They effect life and are not merely focused on financial rewards. Although the great leaders were inspired to make a difference to the world, many began their journey with a quest for power and wealth. Leaders as diverse as Genghis Khan to the CEOs of the major American corporations of the 20th century began with a power and wealth motive and then turned this into a legacy motive. The latter established the

Rockefeller Foundation, Carnegie Endowment and the Gates Foundation.

Improvement They enhance what is on offer today. Although we focus more on the great innovations, many periods of history are filled by leaders whose aim was to consolidate, maintain and refine the gains delivered by others.

Aspirational strategy has the power to unlock people's ambitions. Great strategists have had powerful communication capabilities which they have used to change people and unlock their energy. Such energy can be an enormous force for good or bad.

Aspirational strategies of course rely on the aspiration of the visionary individual strategist. True aspiration-based strategy, in common with inclusion strategies, requires a pure state of mind. Only the Enlightened Strategist can pursue such a strategy, and as a consequence such strategies are fraught with many dangers. Those that use the techniques of aspiration have shown their ability to do enormous good but also enormous harm.

In conclusion, principle is required to guide and temper aspirational strategy.

Principle

In popular culture, principle is about taking a higher position of 'right'. The battle for superior principle is not a battle at all. It involves the search for the right answer and the adoption of the right position, but without righteousness. History shows the power of such strategies. Those who are most effective in claiming the moral high ground have been able to rally their people, dehumanise the target and take what they want.

The ability to take a higher position of right requires either that one possesses a recognised position of right, (which naturally attracts followership), or that one possesses right (and imposes it through force). The use of force requires either a blatant admission of greed or a contest of ideologies. Such forceful strategies combine right and might and lead to the execution of a strategy of destruction.

STRATEGIES OF DESTRUCTION

Three key reasons for strategies of destruction are:

> **Retribution and Signalling** The argument is that if the enemy is not clear on the consequences of attacking us, then we will be vulnerable. The Israelis in their late 20th-century conflict with the Palestinians have been clear on the scale and extent of their wrath and have followed through with violence. This path requires clear signalling of intent to defend and take revenge and then follow through to exact retribution. This path has the potential to lead to a long cycle of attack and counter-attack unless the enemy is annihilated or the spiral of violence is broken through peaceful means.
> **Moral Crusade** The argument is that our way of life has something of superior worth, if not sacredness, that must be preserved. With the rise in ideology, moral crusaders appear and take a path that leads to the age-old practice of destruction. From the 11th to the 13th century, Christian crusaders conducted holy wars against those they labelled 'heathens'. Today, the danger of such strategies can be greater for both sides, because of the existence of highly effective weapons of destruction on both sides; the superior access that again both sides have to each other, and the ability that both sides have to propagate their moral superiority.

Pre-Emption and Persecution The argument is that the enemy should be cut down in his infancy to prevent the greater destruction that will result when the enemy becomes older and strong. Such strategies aim to tackle the fear that the enemy will indeed become too strong or a greed for something that the enemy possesses. To gain popular support for the annihilation of the enemy, the enemy is often dehumanised by the use of labels such as 'cancer' or 'vermin'. This path leads to a system where potential enemies are identified, judged and executed. Hitler conducted an effective campaign against the Jews and convinced enough work colleagues, customers and neighbours of the Jewish community in Germany to begin their annihilation.

The basis for strategies of pre-emptive destruction can come from an accurate calculation that the enemy has the potential to become an abuser on a grand scale. Attila, Genghis and Hitler were all potential grand abusers in the early days of their careers. Pre-emptive strategies would involve a decisive move against such leaders while they are far away from their destructive potential. The implications are far-reaching and dangerous. The problem with such strategies arises from the following:

- The assumption that destruction is the answer.
- The belief that the enemy can be annihilated.
- The belief in one's own propaganda, that it is a moral crusade in some incontrovertible moral sense.
- The belief that the enemy will convert, once defeated, to our way because of our innate superiority.
- The lack of consideration of consequences.
- The conviction that a philosophy of identifying nascent

enemies can be successfully contained. To a predetermined definition of who is an enemy.

Many of the justifications for moral crusades are of course very questionable. One of the misconceptions of such strategies in modern times is the belief that the war will be limited to a fight between professional armies. Potential civilian casualties have been overlooked or underplayed by modern politicians in making their case for war. The predecessors of modern generals and politicians knew that this was not the case and were prepared to pay the price. Genghis Khan, in fact, took exactly the opposite view on civilian casualties. He assumed that he could strike fear into the heart of the enemy and break their resolve to fight. Whether they fought or fled, he was prepared to annihilate their armies, townsfolk and villagers. In today's connected world, the consequences of errors of judgement and of brutality cannot be hidden. The media will reveal the details of death inflicted, the abuse of the conquered and the weaknesses and excesses of the soldiers in the aftermath of victory. War will unveil the inhumanity of man against man and reveal it to the world, through the global media.

The difference between historical examples of strategies of destruction and today's strategies lies in the implications of the phenomena of the type discussed in the first chapter of this work, particularly, the following:

Negligible Secrecy, in fact exposure of intent and failures. The media and media distribution channels, particularly the internet, will expose in graphic detail the nature of brutality whether planned or unplanned.

Negligible Physical Protection The adversary will be able to retaliate effectively even if defeated because of the ease of direct or indirect access to his opponent.

Negligible Protection of Assets The global systems of the world, such as capital markets, payments and communication, will be vulnerable precisely because of their global nature. Such systems, if undermined, even for short periods, will change or even undermine the foundations of Western society.

Today, the aggressor who claims the moral high ground and executes this through a strategy of destruction cannot escape the judgement of the world. As mentioned earlier, a strategy of destruction requires the destroyer to abandon any hope of taking world opinion and support with them. It is a path that is, and will continue to become, increasingly difficult to justify in a world of open distribution of, and open access to, news events. Those that are neither destroyers nor effective strategists will be 'stuck in the middle' of a problem of their own making. Aggressors will have to choose between strategies based on ruthless destruction and those based on winning the mind.

STRATEGIES FOR HIGHER PURPOSE

Strategies for higher purpose are the most appropriate for transforming a cycle of violence into one of peace, a cycle of poverty and stagnation into prosperity, and a cycle of enslavement into freedom. Each of these situations involves the breaking of a long-standing pattern. A critically important precondition for breaking such patterns is 'confession'. Unless both sides are prepared to confess their errors, there is no possibility of forgiveness and agreements can be built only on expediency.

Higher purpose can be built by creating a higher common aspiration. The methods for creating aspiration include the following:

Rise Above the Conflicting Bodies and Identify a Higher Common Position In 1986, in Reykjavik, Iceland, Presidents Gorbachev of Russia and Reagan of America were able to put aside one of the greatest ideological battles of history, which had been accompanied by the greatest build-up of global allegiances and weapons of mass destruction ever seen, to forge a new path for the world.

Determine How to Take Whole and Thereby Minimise Waste and Destruction Superpowers in history have taken cities whole and built allegiances that avoided the killing of the masses. In history's many eras of military-led supremacy, numerous great powers convinced their foes to let them take their lands without a fight. In the era of economic-led supremacy, America controlled 40 per cent of the world's wealth, measured by gross domestic product, without much of a fight.

See an Event as Belonging within a Flow of Events and so React within the Context of the Flow, not just the Event Great leaders who faced the choice of raising the stakes in their battle, but who saw that the stronger flow of history demanded a more peaceful approach included Mahatma Gandhi, Martin Luther King and Nelson Mandela. Each could have led an armed struggle to achieve their ends but decided to take another path.

The Master Strategist approaches an aggressor with the knowledge that the aggression is not a conflict between himself and the self-appointed rival. This recognition is based on a view that the only aggression can be within himself and within the aggressor. The challenge then becomes one of self-control. If the battle for self-control is won, there are no emotional conflicts. Detachment enables the execution of strategies in a dispassionate manner.

EXECUTING THE STRATEGY

Strategy and action are the basis of delivering results. As such, they are highly practical. Modern strategic thinking focuses on concept over action. Action has been relegated to a field the strategist considers more mundane: the field of operations. The reconciliation of the attractive field of strategy and the apparently mundane field of operations has been fraught with difficulties because of the conflicting nature and training of the 'experts' from each field. The modern experts in strategy (with mostly academic backgrounds in economics, politics and behavioural studies) have been largely unable to reconcile their backgrounds and culture with operational experts (with their backgrounds in mathematics). This gap has been addressed by a number of 'execution strategies' that evolved towards the end of the 20th century and the early 21st century, including:

> *For Individuals*, a focus on self-improvement (numerous programmes for creativity and genius), health and fitness (numerous diets and exercise regimes), balance (yoga, t'ai chi) and survival (Chinese kung fu without the 'way', Japanese aikido without the 'do' and various mixtures of ancient martial arts without the 'harmony' or the philosophy).
> *For Business*, a focus on shareholders (shareholder value analysis), activities (activity-based costing), organisational processes (business process re-engineering), value chains and logistics (value chain and supply chain management) and customers (customer relationship management)
> *For National Affairs*, a focus on tax as an incentive tool (direct and indirect taxation policy), flow of money (money supply management), currency (currency pegging and basketing) and capital (efficiency and incentives for capital markets' participation through regulation and deregulation).

For International Affairs, a focus on poor areas (special development zone incentives), concentration of talent and investment (hubs and 'silicon valley' creation), ports and trans-shipment (tax-free ports), trade cooperation (free or open trade areas) and regions (regional economic unity).
For War, a focus on Superpower war (limited nuclear war preparation), positioning in the battlefield (network war), forestalling the enemy (intelligence-based forestalling) and nascent and first strike (pre-emption).

These and many other methods can, or have the potential to, deliver value by translating policy and strategy into practice. However, where some of them fall short is in the creation of a whole view, taking positions based on this view and exercising influence to create specific results.

In the personal dimension, few people develop a view of what they could do to unlock their potential, few take the 'positions' that will make a difference and few pursue the paths that create self-knowledge and mastery. It is easier to let life lead you than it is to lead.

In the corporate dimension, few CEOs form a view of what will make their institutions truly distinctive, few take original positions that will make a difference and few do enough to influence the outcome. It is easier to let the business environment, markets or regulators lead you than to lead them.

In the national political dimension, few presidents and premiers have a clear view of the potential of their country, few take positions that will unlock the potential of their people or create positive change and few influence their countries sufficiently to make a significant difference to the prosperity and development of their people. It is easier to spend time dealing with the politics of governing than it is to lead.

In the matter of war and international affairs, few leaders form a view on the ideal relationship between themselves and their enemies, few take positions that will lead to improvements in world relations and few influence the course that will lead to enhanced peace, prosperity and freedom. It is easier to argue for one's own ideology and welfare, and to avoid conflict or to wage war.

Leaders fail when they fail to form an informed view, fail to take appropriate positions and fail to influence. Leaders invest the resources at their disposal to create results. These resources include the physical resources of people, technology, land and capital, and also the less tangible resources of ideas, intellectual property and relationships. Therefore, one way to see a leader is as an investor in strategies and actions that will lead to the realisation of the outcome for which they have been mandated by citizens.

So, how do we know:

- Who will succeed?
- Which companies will profit from change?
- Which governments will better deliver to their electorate?
- Which international institutions will deliver change?
- Whether a Superpower will remain superpowerful?

In any particular situation to answer these questions we need to look at who has superior view, who has taken appropriate positions and who has the ability to influence the outcome. Only then can we look at the types of positions it is necessary to take and the influence we wish to exert.

View

View is recognised as a critical ingredient of strategy. Data and information must be transformed into a point of view and the quality of this view is a determining factor in the success of our actions. For example, in 2003, did the American government believe that Iraq possessed weapons of mass destruction before they launched their campaign? If so, and if this was a critical factor in the decision to act, how good was their point of view?

The prerequisite for action is the ability to take an informed view. The quality of the view is measured by its accuracy and its differentiation, that is, its height, depth and breadth relative to others. The view must change as the situation changes. It must be alive to remain relevant.

The enemy of view is 'closedness' – resulting in a lack of relevance of the view. Closedness comes from fear. Fear leads to ideology. When individuals close themselves to ideas they become intolerant, and thus are often prepared to fight for their ideology or their expertise. Closedneness operates at many levels:

- When individuals close themselves they stagnate, they lose their ability to grow and adapt.
- When corporations close themselves to ideas they become formulaic in their approach, becoming predictable and therefore vulnerable.
- When governments close themselves they become insensitive to the needs of both their people and their neighbours, and so they begin to decline in relevance.
- When Superpowers close themselves they fail to understand the needs of both their allies and their enemies, and they become ideologically driven.

If such a situation is prolonged, delusion sets in and one

starts to believe one's own propaganda. Ideology leads to superiority complexes or inferiority complexes. Ultimately, this will lead to aggression.

View on its own does not add value. View needs to be transformed by taking positions.

Position

Position is about ownership of some portion of the situation. This requires a stake in the outcome of the view. Position can take many forms, for example, it can be personal, the stance of a person in love or hate for an idea; corporate, the stance of a company in its position regarding products, markets or geographies; governmental, the stance of a government regarding its fiscal policy or its view of who are its enemies and who are its allies. Successful leaders take positions that have the characteristics of surviving organisms. Their positions are alive and fit for the situation.

The enemy of position is a fixed position – a lack of adaptive capability:

- When individuals refuse to adapt to the situation they face they become unfit mentally and physically.
- When corporations refuse to adapt to their environment they lose their position – their customers, profitability and value.
- When governments refuse to adapt to the changing world they lose either their mandate to govern or they resort to oppression.
- When Superpowers fail to adapt to the challenges of the world they become victims of the challengers and/or they become aggressors.

If such a position is prolonged, the path to irrelevance sets in. This path can be a long one, but it ultimately leads to death. The time it takes for death to be reached is dependent on the extent of the changes in the environment. Those with power seldom die without fighting for their preservation. Ultimately, this leads to a defensive-aggressive struggle.

View and position do not add sufficient value on their own. Position needs to be transformed through influence.

Influence

Influence is about intervention, which can take many forms, including personal, economic, societal and political. The superior strategist is not passive, but influences the situation and the environment itself. This influence is based on view and position, both of which must be fit to be relevant. The strategist is effectively an active investor in change.

Influence can range from the subtle to the gross, from the intangible to the forceful, from indirect to direct, from constructive to destructive, from continuous to intermittent. Most people have a habitual pattern for their influencing behaviour. These habits allow others to manipulate them. The Master Strategist exerts influence based on the situation and his purpose.

Strong influence requires control over one's own actions, as well as control over the actions of the other side. Mahatma Gandhi provided an example of the use of a step-by-step control over the situation. He avoided actions that would lead to conflicts spiralling out of control. This happens when each hostile action immediately provokes a more hostile response. Gandhi's mode of engagement proceeded in a series of clearly distinct steps involving a combination of protracted negotiations and direct action.[7] The objective in such situations is to ensure that one controls the actors and thereby maintains control over the escalation process. This is achieved by engaging and withdrawing from confrontation.

At what appears to be the other extreme, in the war between Alexander and the Persian king Darius III, Alexander managed engagement and withdrawal of his troops in a manner that also enabled him to control the situation.

The temptation is to believe that one influences the outcome by taking a position. This can be the case if the size of one's influence on the markets where influence is played out is great. These markets are the political stages such as parliaments, the military battlefields, the televisions in the homes of the people of the world, public stock markets, and the many other forums where value can be exchanged. In large markets, most will take positions that are small relative to the volume of other position takers, and so their influence will be small.

In general, failure to influence results from failure to get involved.

- When individuals fail to influence themselves, their families, communities and enemies they become victims of circumstance.
- When companies fail to influence their customers, competitors, partners and regulators they become second- and third-tier players in their industries.
- When governments fail to influence their citizens and trading partners they become unable to maintain the way of life of their nation.
- When Superpowers fail to influence their allies and enemies they go to war. If such a situation is prolonged, the players cease to be positive participants. They become dictators, victims or irrelevant.

The strength of the circle of view, position and influence determines the strength of the strategy.

BEYOND STRATEGIES OF EXECUTING ACTIONS: CREATING AN ADAPTIVE INTELLIGENT SYSTEM

Levers of Strategy

Theoretically, just as machines have levers that enable the machine to be controlled, situations have levers that enable the situation to be 'controlled'. Given the complexity of situations, no set of levers can be complete. Poor strategy often results from the delusion that we have found the ultimate set of levers. The over-focus and over-long focus on a limited set of levers results in poor adaptation to change.

In a changing environment, that which does not change becomes irrelevant and, over time, dies. This is the law of nature that we witness all around us and is apparent in the history of Mankind. This law is as applicable to entities such as individuals, organisations, investors and governments as it is to plants and animals. Each of these entities has some critical elements that can make it relevant or not. In ensuring one's fitness, the internal and external dimensions must be considered.

There are six key internal elements for an entity: its leaders; its population; physical assets; capital; information and intellectual assets, and its belief system, code, culture or way of doing things. These form one side of the equation.

The other dimension is the external dimension. There are seven key external elements: the physical terrain; information terrain; political, regulatory and legal terrain; military and security terrain; the cultural terrain resulting from the interconnection of subcultures that define a pattern of human intercourse; the financial systems terrain resulting from the composite of credit, payments and capital markets; and other distinct entities with their constituent elements that at first appear to be outside the scope of our consideration, which may be other people, communities, markets, countries and planets.

Each of the elements has its own constituent sub-elements that define its character and are the levers that strategists must deploy to achieve their goals. Herein lies one of the fundamental weaknesses of today's strategic thinking: the belief that the role of the strategist is to pull the internal levers within a predetermined context. The Master Strategist knows his role is to pull the internal and external levers to create the changes required.

Strategic Scenarios and Adaptation: Positioning and Repositioning

To examine the ways in which countries can position and reposition themselves, we may be better off asking Hollywood for the future scenarios rather than the strategy units of most corporations and government departments. Hollywood consistently creates compelling and emotionally charged future perspectives grounded in today's realities. Without this type of perspective it is difficult even to begin the process of creating adaptive strategies. How many strategy units have truly dreamed, dared and analysed to apply the question 'What if' today:

- Sony were to be advised by Charles Darwin on how to evolve their research and development capability into

creative germs that infect the business environment and evolve into winning entities?
- The pharmaceutical industry were advised by the leaders of the British Empire, including Queen Victoria and Sir Robert Clive, on how to maximise their use of the world's diversity?
- The Chinese government were advised by Sun Tzu on how to win without fighting?
- The American government were advised by Genghis Khan on how to achieve their aims in the Middle East?
- The enemies of America were advised by Attila the Hun on how to harass and destroy the will to fight of the American people in their homeland?

The role of strategy is to create change. This change must be fit for the desired result in the context of the environment. For the success to last, the ability to change must be both pre-emptive and responsive. The change must be capable of being both evolutionary and revolutionary. The change must be neither fast nor slow – it must be appropriate.

The Master Strategist 'programmes' the organisation and the environment to create this change in order to achieve an outcome. Although this change happens in a fluid way, to understand it we need to use a simple model that I will call Position–Reposition. This involves morphing the organisation from a current state to a future state, through a series of intermediate positions. It also involves morphing the environment, the external dimension described above, from a current state to a future state, through a series of intermediate positions. To see the whole of this change, we need a clear understanding of the current state, a vision of the future state, and the ability to work backwards from the future to determine the intermediary positions on the journey.

The premise is that any future can be created. The steps in the planning process for 'positioning and repositioning' the organisation require the following considerations:

1   The future must be described imaginatively and clearly at the very beginning so that it appears tangible to those that must strive to achieve it, which may range from just the leaders to the whole entity.

2   Then the existing state should be analysed and understood, so that we have some basis to ascertain how far away we are from the future we desire.

3   The triggers for change – changes in regulation, opening of new markets, technological breakthroughs and others – must then be examined and understood, because these are the tools that help us to accelerate our change.

4   The pathway to the future can then be written from the above, as if we are working backwards through a history that has already happened, preparing the script for our story.

5   The potential results of the endeavour can then be recorded as if they had already happened and the organisation had committed to their achievement.

6   The milestones can then be defined, and the great task broken down into steps, so that it is clear how one will measure the transition from the existing state to the future one.

7   The assets required to achieve success can then be identified and the plan for acquiring them clearly articulated.

Such a strategy formulation process is highly creative and is supported by a technical and operational process. This is not too dissimilar to the process of producing a blockbuster film.

Unfortunately, too many of today's strategies follow a process that can only produce a B-movie.

Survival Strategy: Creating Institutions that Survive and Prosper

The critical realisation for us is that, given the enormous number of entities, levers and potential moving parts at any given time, it is not possible to continually create strategies to respond. Our aim should be to create a system that responds and succeeds. The role of the strategist is therefore to specify the system, design it, mastermind its creation, deploy it, monitor it, refine it, and destroy and rebuild it. Therefore, the Master Strategist is a master at dealing with people and is an organisational and environmental systems engineer. The Master Strategist is the creator of an intelligent, adaptive system.

We will examine the idea of an intelligent adaptive system from three perspectives. Each perspective will provide us with the critical requirements that the Master Strategist builds into the system. The perspectives are interrelated and overlap, and they provide us with the capabilities and attributes that need to be built to create a strategic adaptive entity. The perspectives and the critical requirements are:

1   *To Create the Capability to Learn and Adapt*, by organising the entity so that it operates as an efficient system that learns and adapts.

2   *To Create the Capability to Self-Organise*, by constructing the entity so that it is self-organising and does not require continuous recalibration.

3   *To Create the Capability to Survive and Prosper*, by creating an entity that has the ability to survive and prosper.

These are interdependent requirements. Indeed, they are to some extent sub-sets of each other.

A number of organisms have learnt, adapted, self-organised, survived and prospered. Charles Darwin developed the first coherent scientific theory to explain this success, which he described as the Theory of Evolution. With it we were introduced to new concepts on which to build our understanding of successful organisms, which now includes concepts such as 'struggle for existence', 'variation', 'survival of the fittest', 'natural selection', 'transmission of acquired characteristics' and 'gene pool'.

In this context, we will explore the characteristics of organisms that prosper as a basis for developing strategies for individuals, communities, companies, nations and cross-national entities. By the end of the 20th century, a number of 'organisms' had won:

- **Among Nations**, America emerged as *the* great nation. It spent 7 per cent of its GDP on education and $4,631 per capita on healthcare which were the highest rates in the world. It had the greatest number of people – 166 million – with access to the internet. America also had the mightiest army, won the most Nobel prizes, produced the biggest companies in the world and, with 275 billionaires, had the highest number of the richest category of people. In surveys throughout the 1990s, over 70 per cent of Americans – the highest percentage in the world – said they were very proud to be American just as, during the height of their empire, Rome's citizens considered the greatest prize was to be a Roman citizen.[8]
- **Among Companies**, GE corporation emerged as one of the greatest of companies. Jack Welch restructured its portfolio in the 1980s by forcing decisions either to make the conglomerate's businesses number 1 or 2 in each

industry or to exit. He instituted a series of changes that would produce one of the most aggressively competitive corporations of the century. Six of the major programmes that defined the DNA of the organisation were the 'Workout' initiative to take unnecessary work out of the organisation, 'the Boundaryless Company' initiative to remove barriers among functional, the 'Globalisation' initiative, which aimed to develop international businesses, the 'Services Business Development' initiative, designed to add technology-intensive services to the hardware businesses, the 'Six Sigma Quality' initiative to introduce a zero-defect-type quality into the business, and the 'Stretch Objectives', which were designed to set extraordinarily stretching goals for managers, which in turn drove serial acquisitions. In 2000, GE Corporation delivered revenues of $129.85 billion and net income of $12.74 billion, and the share price grew by approximately 25 per cent per annum. By 2004, GE had 11 businesses, with more than 300,000 employees in 160 countries, and, valued at a market capitalisation of $388 billion, was the world's biggest company.[9]

- *Among Consumer Communities*, Tokyo emerged as the most vibrant. In the 1980s Japan's economy was the envy of the world. Its economy grew at twice the rate of the US, average Japanese stocks traded at over 200 times earnings by 1990 and the average Japanese residence cost nearly 40 times the average annual income earned by a Japanese household. The following decade saw the Japanese stock market, the Nikkei, fall from a high of nearly 40,000 in 1990 to under 13,785 by the end of 2000. However, the most robust consumer society in the world remained the Japanese and Tokyo was its hub.

Tokyo had the largest metropolitan area in the world with 30 million people. The next largest, New York, had 18 million. The average hourly wage was $21.01 in Japan, compared to $12.37 in the United States. The Tokyo consumer was one of the most demanding in the world with the world leaders in consumer electronics – Sony, Panasonic and Canon – leveraging advanced technologies in semiconductors, miniaturisation and product design to provide the most sophisticated gadgets in the world as a test before (sometimes) shipping them to the rest of the world. Factors that reinforced the creation of a superior consumer and supplier included government promotion and protection of the electronics industry and a heavy investment in broadband deployment (100 per cent of Japanese schools were online and they had a PC for every 10 students). As a result, a Japanese customer demands more sophisticated Technology than others. Approximately 90 per cent of mobile phones had cameras, compared with about 20 per cent for the rest of the world, and about 80 per cent of personal computers had embedded TV tuners. Japan is the world's biggest exporter of consumer electronics, but much of its most innovative and exciting electronics are only sold to the domestic market. One of the effects of this (or is it a cause?) is that Japanese consumers are intensely style and status conscious, willing to pay more for better and cooler features and to upgrade their core electronic devices more frequently than others.[10]

- *Among Investing Institutions*, Warren Buffet's Berkshire Hathaway emerged as *the* great investor. At a time when traders bid up stocks, advisors dreamt up complex financial structures for companies and rumours and momentum drove share prices, Berkshire

Hathaway took a 'fundamental' approach to valuing a company by looking for those with low overheads, strong market share, high revenue growth potential and a low share price. Its value per share grew at a compound rate of 22 per cent from $19 to over $41,000 over the 38 years to 2003. Mr Buffet built the company into one with a market capitalisation of $134 billion. In 2000, Mr Buffet was the 14th richest man in the world, and by 2004 had risen to become the second richest, with an estimated net worth of $42.9 billion.[11]

• *Among Creatures*, Man was, of course, still the leader. For many scientists, a species's success is measured by its population size. In which case, the most successful species known to Man is a type of bacterium called SAR-11, which had an estimated population of 240 times a billion billion billion cells floating around in the oceans, compared to about six billion humans. However, the sheer control of the planet by Man could be taken as one measure of leadership. Man's innovation, just in the 20th century, includes the automobile, highways, television, the aeroplane, spacecraft, electronics, the internet, water supply, petroleum and nuclear technology. However, the future of Man may well be linked to a sustainable use of the planet's resources and a co-existence with other species, not with the great breakthroughs that are Man's legacy.[12]

A number of studies have sought to define the characteristics of winners. This endeavour is prone to superficiality, because it focuses on the symptoms. We get better answers by examining the underlying system and understanding what makes it survive and prosper in the face of change.

We will see from the specifications described below, that the intelligent and adaptive institution is not a product of the ego of the strategist.

TO CREATE A STRATEGIC SYSTEM, CREATE THE CAPABILITY TO LEARN AND ADAPT
Genghis Khan organised his army into a machine that would win in the harsh conditions of 12th- and 13th-century Mongolia. His system included heavily armed elite troops, militia-like general troops, an army organised into units of one hundred thousand and ten thousand, not sorted by tribal affinity, as was historically the case, an elite 'Household Guard', with hand-picked commanders, and strict rules of engagement that were clear to all and rigorously enforced. This system of leadership and organisation enabled him to conquer most of the known world of his time. However, in his 'Yasa', his code of honour, dignity and excellence, he warns his descendants that they should not adhere strictly to his system, because if they do, the power of their state will be shattered and come to an end.

To create a learning and adaptive system, the Master Strategist will need to instil a number of key attributes into the entity, namely:

Self-Organisation The entity needs to be able to organise itself in accordance with changing requirements.

Continual Evolution The entity needs to evolve and 'mutate' as the environment changes.

Autonomous Components Each component of the entity needs to be given autonomy within an overall design.

Feedback Loop The entity needs to respond to a rich information system that provides information on internal and external elements.

Flexible Hierarchy The structure of the entity is determined by the need to maximise flexibility and its responsiveness to changes.

Relevance The entity must be ready to adopt new features and change its character in order to stay relevant.

TO CREATE A STRATEGIC SYSTEM, CREATE THE CAPABILITY TO SELF-ORGANISE

Perhaps the most interesting self-organising system is Man himself. Man has transformed himself from a hunter to a villager to a city dweller to a global traveller to a digital agent on the World Wide Web. The ability to organise and to mould an individual's life, a family, a community, a company and larger units is a defining characteristic of Man. Environmental adaptation may be the defining characteristic of Man and may provide the greatest counter-balance to our genetic predispositions.

The principle of self-organisation is relevant to strategists in developing an adaptive organisation. To self-organise, the 'organisational system' will need to evolve ahead of external pressures and imperatives. To then pursue controlled growth, the system will need to eliminate waste and adopt a pattern of behaviour most suited to local requirements.

To create the capability for self-organisation, the Master Strategist will need to instil a number of key attributes into the entity, namely:

Autonomy The entity will be capable of acting of its own accord and in the absence of external control.

Dynamic Operation The entity will evolve its functions dynamically, with no particular time pattern, but will be driven by the need for its operations to be effective.

Fluctuations The nature of the entity will vary as it searches through options until it finds an appropriate state for the environment it faces.

Differentiation The entity will break with its class or cluster to take forms that enable it to strive for superiority.

Order The entity will seek order amongst its constituent elements so that it can perform, and this will emerge from interactions between each of its elements.

Coping with Instability Facing an unstable environment, where change is non-linear, the entity will adapt by making non-linear choices, that is, leaps.

Criticality The entity will be aware of the limits or thresholds of its performance and will be prepared for step changes.

Self-Maintenance The entity will self-correct and continue to perform.

Multiple Equilibriums The entity will recognise the need for many possible local designs, each suited to the local environment.

Adaptation. The entity will track external variations and adapt its functionality accordingly.

Complexity The entity will be able to perform in environments with many concurrent forces with many objectives or possibilities.

Hierarchies Each level of aggregation of activities and functions in the entity will possess self-organising capability.

Growth–Death Each element of the entity will either grow or die depending on the requirements of the entity as a whole.

TO CREATE A STRATEGIC SYSTEM, CREATE THE CAPABILITY TO SURVIVE AND PROSPER

In the controversial area of large-scale trends that may speed up the process of evolution of biological organisms, eight serious candidates have been proposed as the basis of success of future evolution. These are energy intensiveness, evolutionary versatility, developmental depth, structural depth, adaptedness, size and complexity. It is argued that a species with high evolutionary versatility has a wide range of ways in which it can adapt to its environment, and the resultant organisms would be more efficient and better at exploiting their environments. Einstein believed that the system that would help Man survive was a 'supranational organisation'.

To create the systematic capability to survive and prosper, the system will need to possess a number of key attributes. Here are a selection of actions that the Master Strategist can take to assist the entity's chances of surviving and prospering:

> *Preserve Options* End-positions result from the merging of choices. Irreversibility is inherent in the concept of an end-position. The Master Strategist ensures that options are preserved and fixed positions and dead-ends are avoided.
>
> *Maintain System Integrity* Survival requires the ability to change the structure of the system and its networks. Adaptive entities change fluidly whereas solidified entities change dramatically or destructively. The Master Strategist ensures that the intensity of the entity is intact in the face of changes.
>
> *Create Real-Time Holistic Information Feedback* A perfectly refined entity eliminates redundant features and comprises only the essentials. Such a system will also be perfectly interdependent and highly connected externally. Systems with high connectivity are highly sensitive to disturbance. The Master Strategist ensures that a holistic information system provides feedback on change.
>
> *Promote Spontaneous Adaptability* Systems that are able to change their elements and their connections in a fluid manner as they respond to the environment are found to move spontaneously from the chaotic or static to stability. In this balanced state they are also ready to change spontaneously. The Master Strategist ensures that the entity responds spontaneously to the changes.

Add Competition to Increase Adaptability In natural genetics, there appears to be a selective bias towards functions that can support self-organisation to the edge of chaos. Therefore, the Master Strategist builds adaptive and competitive mechanisms to both control and facilitate change.

Influence the Wider Environment Systems alter themselves to maximise adaptability. Organisms do not merely adapt, they create the landscape in which they can survive. Therefore, the Master Strategists empowers the entity to influence the environment not merely to react to it.

Let Resources Flow to Requirements At any point in time, any part of the network can face uneven change requirements. Therefore, resources need to be able to flow freely to the part of the entity that requires resources. Given the finite nature of resources. The Master Strategist ensures that the entity discriminates between requirements to sacrifice the parts in the context of survival of the whole.

Prepare for Step Change The pressure for change grows with the size of the system. Beyond a critical point, which is dependent upon the rate, size and criticality of the pressure, it is no longer possible to achieve adaptive improvement. Therefore, the Master Strategist ensures that once the network has reached a certain size, fundamental changes will be required to preserve integrity.

Prepare for Interdependence and Convergence An entity exists and evolves within an environment that includes other entities that also seek to exist and evolve. Such entities compete for resources and reach an equilibrium in the utilisation of resources that enables them to co-prosper. Individual elements of the entities may consume or be consumed. Where the purpose of the entity class is the same, it is also possible for the entity class to merge. The Master Strategist recognises that such a merger may be required to rationalise the consumption of common resources and to strengthen the surviving class of entities and enables this to happen.

Promote Learning In the transitional state, the system has some relatively fixed and some growing or dynamic areas. Pathways between the dynamic regions allow controlled dissemination of information across the system. Therefore, the Master Strategist ensures that the system learns and passes on lessons along its network.

Winning Using an Adaptive Intelligent System

In the light of the specifications of an Adaptive Intelligent System given above, we should question the role and mode of strategists. Too often strategists preoccupy themselves with narrow questions such as comparison of one product to another, one market to another and one country to another. These are questions for analysts, not strategists.

More appropriate questions would be of the following type:

- *How is the System of Advantages Shifting in the World and How Will that Affect Existing Players?* The system of advantages are those factors that contribute to one country outperforming another, and include wage and cost structures, local consumption of products, ability to manufacture in bulk at the required quality and the ability to generate new product specifications.

   To take a more specific example, for the consumer electronics industry we should consider what is the nature of the shift of economic power in the industry and is it part of a continuum of shifts away from existing players to new ones such as the Koreans and Chinese? Also, how can the US re-emerge as a potential force?

- *How do the Systems of Enterprise Differ between Markets and What are the Implications for those Seeking to Enter from Other Systems of Enterprise?* The system of enterprise encapsulates the factors that lead one market to produce more 'fit' enterprises than another, and include the ability to innovate, to fund ideas, to manage new ventures, to exit these ventures for profit and also the ability to destroy less fit entities.

  To take a more specific example, in emerging markets, what are the systems of enterprise in China and India and which one is most likely to offer us opportunities, given the system of enterprise that we have grown up in?

- *How does the System of Wealth Creation in One Country or Region Compare to Another?* The systems of wealth creation determine the profitable growth of one system relative to another. It includes macro-factors such as the government capability to promote trade, industrial growth, capital markets, entrepreneurship and instructive competition. It also includes micro-factors described above as the system of enterprise.

  To take a more specific example, in the competition of nations, how robust is the European system of generating wealth compared to the new systems that are being shaped in Asia's fastest growing countries? What evolutions are required in the US system of enterprise to remain a leader?

Strategists must probe the nature of the underlying system and seek to understand both how they are developing and how they compare to others if they develop effective strategies.

The task of the Master Strategist is ultimately to build an intelligent system that adapts to the world itself, because this world is changing so quickly that we cannot predict or direct all of the required change. The Master Strategist will use the internal levers to create his adaptive and open organism. He will also use the external levers to influence the environment. The system that results will need to be capable of managing change and relationships so that it becomes a strategic system. This requires the system to have the following change characteristics:

Disruption-Ready At the critical point, any size of disruption can potentially cause any size of effect – it is impossible to predict the size of the effect from the size of the disruption for large systems. Therefore, self-organising disaster recovery capability is required.

Innovation-Assimilation Capable Too high a rate of innovation leads to information loss, chaos and breakdown of the system. Therefore, the execution of change must be managed carefully.

Diversity-Adaptive Entities become familiar with alien entities and either destroy, assimilate or succumb. The ability to adapt to diversity is critical to success. Given the complexity of the world, the ability to extract value from diversity becomes a critical factor in surviving. Since we have experienced only a fraction of the diversity on the planet, and have not yet learnt to assimilate this diversity, we can expect to be surprised by it. Therefore, the ability to use diversity must be promoted.

Exchange and Trade Encouraging Two or more interacting autonomous entities that, in combination, increase growth rates above those of either in isolation will, in the absence of corrupting influences, tend to merge or trade. Therefore, internal and external interactions where the benefits are mutual must be encouraged.

Commercially Disciplined If innovation involves a cost,

then the rate of innovation will be constrained by the payback and its period. This is seen not only in ecological systems, but in economic situations, where risk-profit forms a reduced constraint. Interactions must have a net positive contribution to be sustainable. Therefore, commercial disciplines must be introduced and maintained.

Widespread Networked Learning The number of potentially disruptive events increases exponentially in line with the number of units in a network. Learning by the 'units' in the network enables disruptions to be contained. Learning without widespread dissemination leads to an uneven and weaker total network.

The partial system specification given in the preceding paragraphs on intelligent adaptive systems should illustrate the need for the strategist and leader to distance themselves from the emotion of ownership and focus on the fitness of the entity of which they are merely a steward.

THE DRIVERS OF FAILURE: CORRUPTING THE SYSTEM

All empires and Superpowers come to an end. The might of the Egyptians, the Persians, the Greeks, the Romans, the Byzantines, the Arabs, the Mongols, the Ming, the Tokugawa, the Ottoman and the British came to an end. The American dominance of the 20th and early 21st centuries will also inevitably end. The merchant empires within these great powers also inevitably came to an end. The great global corporations of the 20th and 21st centuries will similarly fade away. The big ideas, however, remain for longer.

Each empire and Superpower has the opportunity to vest in

the next generation a big idea. The fall of empires and Superpowers comes when they are no longer the fittest system for delivering peace, prosperity and freedom. The fall can be a long time in coming, but accelerates as the system becomes more and more unfit. The corruption of its fitness comes from the internal corruption of the system. This has been the cause of the dissolution of countless empires and Superpowers in history. The internal cancers that corrupt the system arise from internal attitudes, power struggles and imbalances:

Focus on the Glorious Past: The Power of Legacy to Prevent Progress Over-focus on past strengths results in a failure to build the assets required to compete with new or 'foreign' entities.

Focus on Personal Projects: The Power of the Initiative Over the Whole Focus is on initiatives rather than on creating a 'system' and a culture of success.

Focus on Heroes: The Power of the Individual at the Expense of the Whole Over-intervention in the system results in a distortion in the adaptiveness and flexibility of the system, harming the ability of the system to survive and prosper.

Focus on Ourselves: The Power of Parochialism Over Scope The failure to think beyond local boundaries and instead to pursue local interests that are at odds with institutional interests.

Focus on Autonomy: The Power of Empowerment to Stop Unity The fragmentation of policy as a result of failure of the components of the system to work together.

Focus on Pleasure: The Power of the Pleasure-Drive Over the Work-Drive The tendency to take what one can, even in an abusive fashion, often overrides the duties to oneself and others.

The common modern causes of corruption of systems from the outside include mis-regulation, support and subsidy of unfit entities, abuse of information and misallocation of public resources.

Remember, there is always an outside. To the individual, the outside may be the organisation. To the organisation, the outside may be the nation. To the nation, the outside may be the region or international community. To the international community, the outside may be the superpower or empire of the time. To the Superpower the outside may be the 'subversive'-'terrorist'-'freedom-fighter', and so we are back to the individual. Indeed, we are back to the idea: the subversive idea, the terrorist idea, the freedom idea. The fight is the fight against or for the mind of others. Remember, there is no such thing as an outside; everything is interrelated. One man's outside is another man's inside.

The cycle of the rise and fall of entities is a natural phenomenon afflicting all entities. Apparently random events cause the right leaders to become the wrong leaders, the right influences to become the wrong influences and the right assets to become the wrong assets. These wrongs are wrong because they are no longer fit to survive and prosper. They become wrong because they do not adapt. Their adaptive capability is corrupted for reasons that are age-old. The root causes can be traced to emotional weaknesses, fear and greed: fear to institute change and greed to horde and gorge on the fruits of success.

In conclusion, in the face of overwhelming assaults from the inside and the outside, the role of the Master Strategist is to create and maintain a strategic system: a system that is intelligent and adaptive, that is fit to win.

In the next chapter, we will examine the types of strategic paths that need to be pursued to break through our current barriers in thinking about strategy.

FUTURE PATHS FOR STRATEGY

'The events in the world result from causes that we do not see or understand. The interrelatedness of these causes has consequences that we do not understand. Our actions cause outcomes that we do not understand. The result is chaos. A better future requires us to better understand the nature of things today.'

The Book of Power, Purpose and Principle

THE GREAT OPPORTUNITIES OF OUR TIME

The challenges posed in Chapter one of this book concerned the type of world we live in, and hence the nature of our existence. We also considered the potential present in each of the Seven Shaping Phenomena. Each of them offers us numerous opportunities, including the chance to create:

- The Age of Miracles *or* the Age of the End of Times
- The Age of Ideas *or* The Age of Propaganda
- The Age of Silicon Valleys *or* The Age of Destructive Competition of Valleys
- The Age of Super-Science *or* the Age of the Science of Mass Destruction
- The Age of Global Prosperity *or* The Age of Self-Interest and Protectionism

- The Age of Capitalism *or* The Age of Capitalists
- The Age of Higher Consciousness *or* The Age of the Battle of Ideologies
- The Age of Hyperpower *or* The Age of the End of Superpower
- The Age of Fast Wars *or* The Age of Continuous War

Can so many possibilities be present in our today? The answer is that there are many more possibilities than we can imagine. It is important not to get over-focused on these seven phenomena. This, too, will limit us. Our ability to imagine, develop and execute appropriate strategies is the only limitation we must face if we are to realise the best of the potential opportunities. We need a revolution in how we develop strategies, and how we develop our strategists, if we are to attain the more positive paths that arise from the changes in the world.

STRATEGIES OF THE FUTURE

So, the seeds of our future are present in our today. The shaping phenomena give us an idea of the potential choices we have. However, the shape of that future is subject to the chaotic nature of the consequences of these shaping phenomena. With analytic-intuitive leaps we can identify some of the most important points along these paths, but there is no guarantee of our ability to do so. Hence, there is a need to create a system that is itself strategic in its response to change.

The strategic system does not exist in isolation of the architect-master-creator of the system, the Master Strategist. Nor does it exist independently of the environment in which the strategic system and its architect operate. In staying fit for its purpose, the strategic system will need recalibration. The recalibration may be gradual or shocking, and these changes will also affect the environment itself.

The unusual explorations of history led to the great branches of today's sciences. Alchemy fed into chemistry, astrology into astronomy, cabbalism into mathematics, and memory systems and labyrinths into libraries and, ultimately into computing and information management. Many of the great figures of the Western scientific revolutions of the 16th and 17th centuries started and maintained an interest in what now appear to be the less rational fields. Johannes Kepler (remembered chiefly for articulating the three laws of planetary motion) practised astrology; Isaac Newton (the philosopher and scientist famous for the three laws of motion and the law of universal gravitation) was a part-time alchemist; Gottfried Leibniz (famous for inventing differential and integral calculus) was interested in hieroglyphic and cabbalistic notation; and Matteo Ricci (the 16th-century Italian Jesuit priest who taught in China) explored labyrinths and memory systems. The risk we face today is that we now pursue a far shallower exploration of our world, which is based on the discoveries of the past, and so we fail to explore more unusual paths ourselves.[1]

We must re-examine our strategic approach: Master Strategists need to examine a number of fundamental questions in order to shape or adapt to a complex-chaotic situation and environment. The critical topics that will act as the impetus behind reaching the next level of breakthrough thinking include:

- The mind
- Transactions and relationships
- Resources and assets
- Time

- Interconnectedness
- Strategy as an adaptive state
- The role of Mankind

Mastery of these topics will help to raise the level of peace, prosperity and freedom in the world. In the wrong hands, however, they will contribute to raising the level of conflict, poverty and enslavement. Hence, tomorrow's liberators and despots may well be those that develop mastery of such fundamental breakthroughs. Big changes arise from big ideas. One of the earliest big ideas – 'trade' – may have arisen to support the building of social relationships between tribes. It has become one of the most potent forces for changes in the balance of economic power. One of the early modes of Man, living in harmony with nature, gave way to the big idea of Man 're-modelling nature' through the building of groups of huts to create villages, fixed structures that changed the skyline, irrigation systems that changed the flow of rivers and dams that contained rivers. Battling and waging war is as old as man but the big idea of 'annihilation' is relatively new and has led Man to subdue or abandon his sense of remorse in the name of a bigger cause.

In the past, great strategic ideas have also been articulated by great strategists from all over the world. Sun Tzu's *The Art of War*, the Indian classic the *Bhagavad Gita*, Miyamoto Musashi's *The Book of Five Rings*, Machiavelli's *The Prince* and Clausewitz's *On War*, all spoke of the secrets of strategy. A deeper examination, however, revealed that these were books not just about the secrets of strategy, but more about the secrets of life.

We will now examine how each of the topics for breakthrough listed above can be the seed of a big idea that, in the future, can change the nature of strategy.

Future Strategic Paths

ONE: THE BATTLE FOR THE MIND

One interpretation of history is that it shows us that attack is the best form of defence. According to this view, history shows us that the Romans could not appease the barbarians, the Chinese could not appease Genghis Khan and the Europeans could not appease Hitler. Therefore, many posed the question, is not a war of the type launched by the US Bush Administration in 2003 against Iraq the best way to crush an enemy before the enemy becomes too strong? Such a question cannot be answered using existing methods of strategy analysis. Increasingly, we need to pursue a more sophisticated line of enquiry to find the answer to this and other such critical questions, including:

- Is political strategy essentially about success at war? Is it not more effective to kill the enemy when he is weak, and are the alternatives not merely forms of appeasement?
- Is corporate strategy essentially about success at competing?
- Is personal strategy essentially about winning fame, fortune or power?

We may well need to move beyond questions that are so focused on the win–lose equation. Leaders find many reasons to wage war, but the roots of conflict are ultimately about fear and greed. These feelings are of course highly personal to the leaders who wish to wage the war. However, war can only be prosecuted if these emotions are also instilled in the hearts and minds of the populace. Hence, the first step in waging war is often to instil fear and greed into the minds of the people and to incite hatred and lust. So, leaders do wage a battle for the mind – the minds of their own people. Unfortunately, leaders are tempted to wage a limited war for the minds of their enemy and a prolonged war for their 'body', the land.

To answer the fundamental questions about whether to wage war in the future, we will need to understand the art of the battle for the mind. The focus of this area of strategy will be on understanding how to win without fighting. Understanding that we face the choice of either needing to annihilate the enemy or succumbing to them will force other paths to be explored. These paths will take the form of stalemate based on mutual threat; compromise based on the need for peaceful co-existence; acceptance based on mutually beneficial exchange and adaptation.

The battle to win the mind is not necessarily fought in one round. The preliminary rounds may involve using other strategies: competition, disruption and domination. These power plays may be part of the preliminary signalling of serious intent. However, since such strategies are essentially about conflict if they are followed through, they will weaken the will to battle for the mind. The weak strategist will succumb to the possibility of taking the land by force and will forgo the more peaceful way of taking the mind. History shows us the seductive grip on conquerors of the power possibility.

The three pretexts in which to conduct the battle for the mind are as follows:

Pre-Mass-Cognitive A strategy of pre-mass-cognitive action, that is action before the mass can perceive the possibility of action, involves no enemy. It requires the Master Strategist to identify potential battlegrounds, rivals and enemies so that he can lay the seeds of mutually beneficial exchange, before enmity develops and long before conflict develops. Thus potential problems are addressed before either side becomes aware of the potential for rivalry. Mutually beneficial exchange can take place with goods, services, peoples and cultures. Failure to pursue this strategy effectively leads to strategies of pre-emption.

Pre-Emptive A strategy of pre-emption requires the forestalling of someone who is now the opponent or enemy. This requires the strategist to communicate his intent to engage and to bear the consequences – costs, casualties and long-term enmity. Such a communication should not be regarded as the end-game. If effective, such a communication can buy the time needed to attempt a more peaceful strategy. Of course, pre-emptive strategies can go well beyond communication and can involve intervention. If a limited intervention is successful, the strategist may still be able to withdraw and re-group in order to attempt a more peaceful strategy. If the mind of the opponent has not been understood, the strategy will backfire and may lead him to see our communication and limited intervention as weakness, causing him to take more dramatic actions against us. Failure to pursue such strategies well leads to strategies of pretence.

Pretence A strategy of pretence requires a pretence, a falsehood, to intervene and take control of a situation, in order to buy time to achieve some other purpose. This other purpose may or may not be to determine how to win the mind. The strategist must find a suitable pretence that will have sufficient credibility with the enemy as well as his own allies, allowing him to take control of a situation for enough time to win the mind of the enemy. This strategy runs the risk that the leaders will enjoy the fruits of their success and will seek to abuse or keep the asset which they have taken control of. The failure to pursue such strategies effectively leads to battles beyond the mind – battles to destroy.

The Master Strategist will see what others cannot yet see and will move before conflict is imminent. He must be able to move:

- From communicating to convincing.
- From employing methods that psychologically undermine the enemy's will to fight to working to build a common purpose.
- From engaging in mutually beneficial trade to turn the enemy into customers to turning the enemy into employees.
- From offering better enjoyment from the consumption of the product to offering something that more fundamentally enhances life.
- From providing aid to providing self-development capital and know-how.
- From selling products to teaching how to become self-sufficient.

The battle for the mind is fought from three positions: a position of fear, a position of greed and position of altruism. Those that approach the battle from a position of fear feel that without it we risk a battle for the land with dire consequences on both sides. Those that come from a position of greed feel that it is the most efficient way to win the land, win the value and win a followership. Those that come from an altruistic position understand that it is the way to create a more sustainable and prosperous planet.

For politicians, the challenge should how to win the mind so as to not waste the body of their army. For corporations, the challenge should be how to win loyalty to their brand and product or service so they can avoid wasting their resources fighting competitors in price wars. For individuals, the challenge should be how to win control over their own mind so as to save themselves from the suffering that comes from fear and greed.

Success in the battle for the mind is achieved when one's own mind is conquered. In this state, one lacks the fear, anger and hatred that leads to destructive war. If one also overcomes greed, lust and malice the other root cause of destructive wars is avoided. The dispassionate state allows a more detached assessment of the situation and therefore less emotive strategies. As a result, strategies can be pursued so that rivals can co-exist, become co-dependent and then merge with us. To achieve this, the assumptions, beliefs and values of both sides must be changed. Strategists capable of achieving such results will have a deep understanding of history, society, culture and human behaviour as well as the mind – theirs and others.

TWO: STRATEGY AS TRANSACTIONS AND RELATIONSHIPS

A fundamental dilemma is that often we find ourselves in circumstances where there is no clear explanation for the extent of the enmity towards us, so what strategy should be adopted to solve such situations? The argument is that surely, the attack on Pearl Harbor in 1941, the attack on 11 September 2001 on the Twin Towers in New York, the regular suicide bombings in Israel since the 1980s are inexplicable, other than to say they are heinous crimes committed by heinous people? The questions posed include:

- From a political perspective, we are often posed the question: is the reason our enemies attack us not inexplicable and are not their methods truly heinous?
- From a corporate perspective, is it possible to create value given there are too many people competing for a share of the customer's wallet?

• From a personal perspective, is it possible to remain centred, to keep our relationships positive and stay away from those that would harm us and ours?

Such questions cannot be answered using existing methods of strategy analysis. Increasingly, we need to pursue a more sophisticated line of enquiry.

When we see outcomes, we should look for a cause. This will help us to get a better understanding of why and it will stop us blaming chance and demonising the enemy. It will enable us to see the role that we – as well as other factors – played in the things that go well and not so well for us. We can look at each cause-and-effect as a transaction. Hence, everything can be viewed as transactional, because there is always a cause and a subsequent effect. The role of the strategist is to determine the transactions required to achieve a desired result. Transactions have a quantitative and a qualitative element, that is, simply put, how much was executed and how well it was executed. Transactions are executed within the bounds of time and space, that is, simply put, over what time they were executed and what distance. Therefore, for any particular situation and environment, strategy is about the strength, extent and quality of our action and the time over which we act. Our (trans)actions will be either appropriate or not.

Transactional strategy can be conducted by giving importance to non-mutually exclusive frameworks or points of reference:

Existential Under this approach, each individual transaction matters. The focus is on the present and on every individual element of existence. Every instance has importance, because every instance involves transactions. The role of the strategist is to develop mastery over the moment. This mastery enables awareness of the nature of existence, which enables everything to be understood and dealt with.

Relationship Under this approach, each series of transactions matters because each series builds a relationship. The emphasis is placed on relationships and the role of the strategist is to develop relationships. The value of the relationship can be determined by the cumulative value – quantitative and qualitative – of the transactions. The relationship can be physical, emotional, spiritual and financial or commercial.

Communal Under this approach, the transactions of the entity matter. It places the emphasis on the entity. For any given situation and environment, the role of the strategist is to determine the transactions required within an entity so that it is fit to achieve its objectives.

Trade Under this approach, the transactions between entities matter. It places the emphasis on external transactions. The role of the strategist is to determine the transactions between the entity and other entities so that the objectives of the entity are achieved.

Holistic Under this approach, all transactions matter because everything is interrelated and interconnected. It recognises the relationship between the individual and all transactions. Boundaries are no longer limiting factors because there is an acceptance that all things are interrelated. This acceptance provides the beginning of the breakdown of boundaries. We will examine this approach in more detail later when we discuss of the Strategy of Interconnectedness.

The elements described above are part of a journey in developing mastery over events. They have too often been seen as methods that stand alone and are self-sufficient. The mastery of transactions opens up the potential to exert the greatest influence over events. The transactional strategist becomes aware of the importance of each interaction, understands the cause-and-effect of each interaction, and thereby comes to an understanding of the nature of things.

Exponents of transactional strategy cover a wide range of people, including religious leaders and currency traders. Around the 6th century BC, the Buddha practised the observation of the movement of his breath, called Vipassana meditation, to transcend the body, the emotions and the mind. It is said that this gave him deep insights into the interactions between all things and their fundamental nature. In 1997, George Soros studied the nature of peoples, regimes and markets and this gave him insights into the transactions required to move these entities. It enabled him and his team to precipitate the collapse of Asian markets and the British Pound.

The methods by which transactional strategy can be carried out are wide-ranging and varied, and include internal methods such as contemplation and meditation and external methods that allow us to design the type, sequence, timing, quality and quantity of transactions. The external methods include diplomacy, trade, threats, battles and wars in personal, corporate and political contexts. Strategists will become masters of interaction through their study of themselves, their environment, their relationships, their communities, societies and their trades. Strategists will need to fuse all these things into an understanding of the relationship between cause-and-effect. To achieve this, strategists will become mathematicians who study chaos theory and meditators who study the flow of the breath and the energy in the body.

THREE: TRANSFORMING THE VALUE OF RESOURCES

As discussed earlier, a commonly held assumption is that, at any point in time, the resources available to us are limited and so we must compete for these resources or limit our choices. Hence, the argument that, ultimately, we must fight for oil, fight for grain, fight for capital, fight for talent, fight for everything. Such issues cannot be addressed using existing methods of strategy analysis. Increasingly, we need to pursue a more sophisticated line of enquiry to find the answers to challenge fundamental assumptions, such as:

From a Geo-Political Perspective, surely the poor will stay poor regardless of what we do because there is insufficient aid available to save them from their despot's wars, famines, diseases and cultural traps?

From a Political Perspective, in the face of shortages of critical natural resources, such as oil, surely we should either cut back our consumption or we should seize the scarce resources for a fairer allocation?

From a Corporate Perspective, having understood our strengths and weaknesses and the basis of our past competencies, surely we should maximise the leverage of what we have?

From a Personal Perspective, our capabilities are limited, our opportunities are few, our competitors are naturally better than us, surely we should settle for less?

Flawed thinking leads to an over-focus on what we have and therefore an over-focus on competing. This finite resource approach results in strategies that seek to exploit situations based on the view that resources and therefore choices are limited. As a result, strategy becomes a game of prioritisation and resource allocation. The result is that we fit what we have to the situation at hand. The resulting strategies also tend to protect rather than expand.

In the future, we will need to transform assets so that their impact and their value is transformed. The types of resource transformation are:

Magnification The objective is to magnify the influence of our resources by using the resources of others. Under this approach, we make others into our agents rather than set up competing networks.

Stretch The objective is to increase the life of the asset. Under this approach, we invest in making the asset more durable and more relevant.

Intensity The objective is to increase the intensity with which the resource performs. Under this approach, we increase the concentration and productivity of our resources through training and motivation.

Ingenuity The objective is to increase the problem-solving ability and the resourcefulness of our resources. Under this approach, we enhance the ability of our resources with methods and techniques that enhance their ability to solve complex problems and identify and use resources effectively.

Functionality The objective is to increase the number of things our resources can be used for. Under this approach, we increase the capability of the resource to make them more able and multi-functional, that is, more able to do more things.

Composition The objective is to change the inherent elements of our resources. Under this approach, we change the mix of our resource pool or we change the composition of an individual resource.

Organisation The objective is to change the way our

resources are deployed and controlled. Under this approach, we change the orientation of our resources so that they are better able to decide, act and work together.

The transformation of what appears to be limited resources into significantly more valuable ones can be likened to the dreams of the alchemists of the 16th century, who sought to transform base metals into gold. When the transformation of resources is achieved and mastered, the strategist becomes an 'alchemist'. This 'strategic alchemy' can be applied by the strategist to:

An Ecology We are used to ecological change with rivers becoming lakes through dams, oil becoming car fuel, ice caps becoming oceans, plains becoming deserts, forests becoming savannahs, jungles becoming plantations and the ozone layer developing a hole. The strategist uses alternative solutions that prevent the depletion of the ecology. This requires the application of technology, capital, physical effort and, most importantly, ideas.

An International Scene The strategist's task is to transform a situation from warring to peaceful, dictated and closed to open and free, and unevenly developed to developed and prosperous. This requires the transfer of assets across boundaries, for example through travel and tourism, the migration of people, the building of global factories, the international selling of products and services and global investments. This is only possible if there is an understanding of mutual dependency. The strategist will transform warring assets with knowledge of peace, poor assets with knowledge of wealth generation, and closed assets with institutions that establish and protect freedom.

A Nation The strategist's task is to transform the national situation from warring to peaceful, dictated to free and poor to prosperous. This requires a range of methods that turns enemies into collaborators, turns a mass population into a workforce and into consumers, turns the enterprising into entrepreneurs, turns the educated into skilled pools of engineers and architects, turns barren land into silicon valleys and hubs to concentrate knowledge, capital, talent and opportunity, turns waste land into factories, and turns relationships into import and export markets.

An Organisation The strategist in the organisation applies the methods of multiplying the value of resources to people, machines, buildings, products and relationships. The outcome is to enable the organisation to achieve results that go beyond the conventional view of what such resources can achieve. When successful, the cost reductions and revenue increases from the organisation's resources are enhanced beyond the organisation's com petitors. Additionally, and more importantly, the institution is able to make a much greater impact on the world.

An Individual The strategist's task is to transform the individual through methods that develop the individual's capacity to unlock his potential. This requires the individual to be carefully selected, since not all will be willing to be challenged and tested physically, emotionally, mentally and spiritually, to be educated to a breadth and depth in ancient and modern content, necessary to be able to translate data and information into insights, foresights and wisdom, and thus be able to tackle increasingly difficult issues.

To summarise, to implement such strategies, the strategist will use information, money, science and technology and physical force. Strategists will become 'alchemists' who transform the potential of people, resources and institutions, thereby also transforming the impact and financial value of these resources. To achieve this we will need strategists with sufficient understanding of the relationship between people, organisations and the environment and the ability to use transforming methods.

FOUR: TAKING CONTROL OF TIME

In most of our strategic thinking, time is either ignored or, at best, looked at as a finite concept, that is, time is running out. According to this view, time is a fixed factor and we can only be beaten by it. Our arrival on the battlefield can be too late, as can our offer of peace, and the launch of our product, and our apologies can be too late to win back our loved ones. Such issues cannot be addressed using existing methods of strategy analysis. Increasingly, we need to pursue a more sophisticated line of enquiry to challenge a number of fundamental assumptions, such as:

If You Are a Political Strategist, you will know that it takes longer for a nation to become prosperous than it does for a government to lose an election. Therefore, under this time-limiting view, in the short term, if we are poor, we will remain poor, and it would be better, surely, to curtail our ambitions and focus on lesser objectives with more chance of delivering success?

If You Are a Corporate Strategist, you will know that it takes longer to deliver growth and value and catch up with a market leader than it does to miss a quarterly returns forecast. Therefore, under the limited view, surely, the answer is to take measured steps to improve our performance?

If You Are a Seeker of Personal Improvement, you will know it takes a lifetime to master meditation, t'ai chi or yoga, to get rich, become wise. For most people, the real question

rapidly becomes: why bother? Surely, shortcuts can be found
– idiot's guides to science, management in 15 minutes,
power yoga, drugs . . .

Ancient strategists understood the importance of time
and timing. Alexander the Great marched his troops throughout the night to surprise his foes. Genghis Khan moved with a
speed that scared his enemies into flight. In the 20th century,
business came to understand the importance of being first too.
In the 1980s, the Japanese car-manufacturers and consumer
electronics companies built new models so quickly that the
prevailing market leaders in the US and Europe could not keep
up. At that time and still today, the usual strategic battle has
been to be first to market.

In the future, we will need to see time as something that can
be controlled like any other factor to gain advantage. Time will
be used in strategies in the following ways:

Timing Strategies fail because they are too late or too soon.
The objective of using timing as a strategy is to find the most
appropriate time. The strategist must decide on the timing
from what appears to be a sea of potential times to solicit a
specific time to act. The result is that we prevail at a point in
time.

Frequency This means determining the timing in a series of
times. The strategist must decide on each action so that
products capture the market, troops advance successfully on
an enemy position and government aid meets the people's
needs. The outcome is that we prevail over sustained time.

Momentum Momentum is created when the strategist
makes a time critical and, as a result, makes an event likely
to succeed. In effect, the strategist 'accumulates time' and
applies it at a specific moment. This 'accumulation' is the

result of concentrating impact. The outcome is that resistance appears futile at that point in time.

Suddenness This is the creation of the unexpected moment. The strategist must make the opposition feel that their timeframe is irrelevant and force a change of pace onto events. The result is to prevail through surprise.

Lapse The strategist must cause the time counted on by others to pass without consequence. The result is to prevail because others lose the moment.

Momentous Moment This is the creation of a specific moment. The strategist must have a sense of the situation and environment and be able to create a moment that becomes a crystallising or defining moment for people. The strategist must make other time irrelevant to make a particular time most important.

Pre-Time This means to be ahead of time. The strategist must see the apparently natural timing of things and be ahead of time. The outcome is to pre-empt the timing of others.

Time can be used to:

Counter Force Newton explained that force is a product of 'mass' and 'acceleration'. In the application of force as a strategic resource, force is a result of the amount (or mass) of resource and the application (or acceleration) of that resource. However, the important insight for the application of strategy is that time can compensate for force. Time is independent of resource. If we can control time, we can compensate for a lack of resource. For example, we can apply our resource at the perfect time to catch our opponent unawares and/or cause him to apply his force too late.

Create Positive Efforts Time can turn potentially negative outcomes into positive ones. It can enable us to pre-empt the rise of malignant forces, avoid the waste of bad timing, such as untimely, infrequent or lapsed timing, and create impact through deciding the timing, the frequency or the moment correctly.

Control Others Time can allow us to control others. With appropriate timing, we can make others waste their efforts, miss the moment, succumb to our suddenness and become irrelevant.

Extract Value The superior use of time allows us to take value from any situation and environment. For example, we can be on the field of battle at the right time, capture the moment, create the appropriate moment, surprise our rivals, pre-empt others and control the relevance of others.

Strategists will become adept at controlling time. They will be sensitive to the situation and the environment, and possess the ability to manoeuvre to control the use of theirs and their rival's resources. The control of time is a complex undertaking because it requires the possession of accurate information on the rival's resources, position and intentions as well as one's own. Therefore, the use of time in strategy will become an asset available to all but mastered by few.

FIVE: INTERCONNECTEDNESS

By the early 21st century, because of the development of expertise in many narrow fields, we showed little capacity to develop a more whole view of things. For example, at the beginning of the 21st century, most people thought that the world was segregated in a way that meant the privileged could afford to live in the 'First World', sell to most of the 'Third World' and ignore Africa. Similarly, governments of the leading nations protected their national interests and companies fought hard to protect their intellectual property rights in the face of what they saw as pirate nations. Many investment analysts became experts and advised on the movement of the capital of the world based largely on views of commodities, companies and industries. They ignored the changes that were making their narrow expertise less relevant, such as the rapid rise of disruptive events, the convergence of technologies, the new pattern of relationships between nations and the interconnected nature of things.

It is clear that there is a need for a more complete view across the fields of policy, government, commerce, investing and personal matters that cannot be addressed using the prevailing methods of strategy analysis. Increasingly, we need to pursue a more sophisticated line of enquiry to find the answers to challenge fundamental assumptions, such as:

- We support globalisation, free trade and open capital markets because those are what have made us successful; they are the circumstances under which we win. Surely, others should open their borders and compete with us? We know we will win.
- The answer to strategy is differentiation, cost or focus. If each of my corporation's divisions does one of these three things surely we will win in market competition? Surely, game-changing events are too far away to matter?
- I win, you lose is the natural order of things. It is a fact that individuals are unequal. If we focus on one of our key strengths – our mental performance or our physical performance – surely, we will be more successful than others?

The tendency of modern strategic approaches is to limit the scope of enquiry in the above ways. This is a result of many factors, including the limitations of our current individual development, emotional failing and technology limitation. We do not have the methods and techniques to examine our reality, we do not have the will to enter a broad, deep and complex line of enquiry, and we do not have the machines to process the information we can gather. In the future, a well-developed strategy of inter-connectedness will help us to better understand the impact we have on the world and recognise the link between the causes of events. As such it enables us to see patterns of causes and events.

An approach to strategy based on interconnectedness can be categorised very simply into three types:

Simple Equation Strategy This approach, which pre-dominates today, simplifies situations into a limited number of variables. Only identified and understood variables are included.

Simple Equation Plus an 'X' Factor This approach simplifies situations into a limited number of variables, but recognises that there is an unknown factor that can make the result turn out to be other than what is imagined. Such approaches are often used, and range from simple sensitivity analysis (the sensitivity of the result to changes in individual variables) to scenario analysis (the result based on different scenarios built from a combination of variables) to risk analysis (the result based on analysing the impact of risks that alter the situation).

Chaos Theory This approach holds that, built into all events, is a knock-on effect that we cannot predict. The theory is at a nascent stage and looks for patterns in what appear to be random behaviours. As yet, it has not been translated into strategic methods.

A number of hurdles have to be overcome before we can move to an approach to strategy based on inter-connectedness. The hurdles are based on assumptions that form the basis of the world view of strategists and are as follows:

> *The Assumption of Dependency* Such strategists assume that there is a one-way dependency. Generally, they are in dominant positions in their countries, industries or environments. This leads them to assume that they initiate change. Consequently, in their planning models, they subconsciously consider themselves the most important factor in their deliberations.
>
> *The Assumption of Co-Dependency* Such strategists assume that there is a two-way dependency, and that their role is to establish strategies for dealing with a series of two-way interactions: between customers and themselves, suppliers and themselves, employees and themselves, allies and themselves, enemies and themselves.
>
> *The Assumption of Multi-Dependency* Such strategists assume that there is a multi-way dependency, and that it is critical to examine communities of interests such as coalitions in a war, segments of customers and regions of the world.

In the absence of the computing power to process the many variables in our environment and the awareness described in the stories of the enlightenment of the Buddha, there is a need to develop the qualities and methods that will enable strategists to examine interconnected cause-and-effect in a more sophisticated manner and develop strategies based on this understanding. A more interconnected view will need to examine and use the following causes:

Triggers Trigger events crystallise an outcome by causing an event to occur before the time estimated according to conventional views of the trend line. The 1979 seizing of the American Embassy in Iran, perhaps more than almost any other event, crystallised a global awareness of a more 'fundamentalist' Islam. Master Strategists will trigger events rather than follow trends.

Ambitions We need both analytic and intuitive ways to examine the ambitions of leaders. We need to be able to explain the links between reason, objective, purpose, vision, aspiration and formal decision-making methods. For example, the decisions to build pyramids, computers, empires are amongst the most obvious and dramatic evidence of our leaders' ambitions. Strategy formulation without an understanding of the ambitions of our opponents leads to a failure to understand one of the most important drivers of strategy. Master Strategists will have a clearer understanding of their own and their rival's ambitions.

Actions We frequently focus on the actions of others without looking at how our actions caused them. Islamicists pointed to the action of the UN in establishing Israel in 1947 as the cause for widespread hatred of Americans in the Islamic Middle East. Obsessed with their own hatred, most people fail to seek the causes for hatred their enemies feel for them. Master Strategists will have more sophisticated ways to examine action and consequence. They will understand that actions cause other actions.

Spontaneous Events Spontaneous events are causes for which we have no explanation, given our present under-standing of the world. For example, apparently spontaneous and therefore disruptive events include natural disasters, stock market crashes, surprise election results and assassinations. Master Strategists will take into account the potential role of disruptive forces and will focus more on adaptation than prediction.

Natural Laws Natural laws seem to create momentum in a certain direction. As we break new boundaries of science, our understanding of natural laws grows. So, we can begin to better appreciate the predominant direction of the force of nature. The Master Strategist will better understand the nature of things, the 'natural' direction of things and use this direction to create a greater force behind his strategies.

Similarly, strategists forming a view of inter-connectedness will also need to examine and use effects. Effects fall into the following categories:

Multiplier A multiplier effect occurs when one cause results in an unexpectedly large number of effects. To achieve a multiplier effect, the strategist will need to enlist others in responding to an event, either consciously or inadvertently.

Domino A domino-effect occurs when a cause leads to a chain of effects, where each effect almost inevitably triggers another, which in turn quickly triggers another effect and so on. To achieve this, the strategist must construct causes that will lead to a chain reaction. He needs to be able to create momentum, understand timing and control time sufficiently to maintain a link between the individual events. A successful domino-effect creates the psychological impact of 'inevitability' in the minds of participants.

Programmed A programmed effect is one that is pre-determined to take a certain form given a specific cause. The strategist must control the main factors involved in order to predetermine the impact of a cause on a situation. Given the role of uncontrollable factors in any situation, it would be more accurate to say that the role of the strategist is to create near-programmed effects or the illusion of totally programmed effects.

Reaction This takes the shape of instinctive or compulsive responses to causes. The strategist must consider the nature of things so that the underlying causes are understood and, where necessary, select causes that lead to specific required reactions.

Spontaneous Spontaneous effects are causes for which we have no explanation given our present understanding of the world. To create spontaneous effects, the strategist would need the capability to trigger chaotic events. Chaotic events are ones whose root causes are not easily identifiable. This is a dangerous strategy, since it leads to unpredictable outcomes. Examples of such triggers include dramatic reductions in price in a high sales season or the launching of a pre-emptive strike against a marginal enemy in order to send a message to our more formidable enemies that we are unpredictable and mighty.

There is a highly analytic part to practising strategies of interconnectedness, since, to be effective, the strategist must understand the underlying series of causes-and-effects. When super-computers are available on the desktop we will be a step closer to developing some of the ingredients for this type of analysis. In the meantime, systematic data gathering, pattern-recognition, intuition and imagination will play a critical role in this form of strategy. In the more ancient traditions of meditation, such strategists were referred to as students of the 'essence of all things'. Master Strategists were said to be those that understood the links or, as the old masters of meditation said, the gaps between events, thus enabling them to see the interconnectedness of all things and so better to discern the consequences of action.

SIX: STRATEGY AS ADAPTIVE STATE

Will America survive the first two decades of the 21st century as the leading Superpower of the world? Will China rise to be the main counter-balancing force? Will India rise above its politicians' ineffectiveness to unlock the potential of more than a billion Indians? Will Europe become merely a great place to taste the fruits of history and culture? Will Africa continue to remain in plight? Will the Japanese rise again to make a mark on the world's markets following their decline at the end of the 20th century? Such questions cannot be answered using existing methods of strategy analysis. Increasingly, we need to pursue a more sophisticated line of enquiry to find the answers to such fundamental questions as:

- Can Superpowers, empires, high-performing countries maintain their strategy of greatness in perpetuity?
- Can high-performing companies maintain their strategy of delivering superior returns beyond the life of their visionary leader?
- Can individuals who excel at one thing continue to excel if we take them out of their field of success?

History reminds us that a great past provides no assurance of future greatness. The history of political empires, merchant empires and great performers all tell the same story. The formulae of the past provide some indications of what it took to survive in a different time. Indeed, 'formulae' conveys the sense of superimposing a static framework on a moving reality. Yet strategic theorists continue to promulgate formulae, even though it is the very use of formulae that is the enemy of survival. New circumstances call for new frameworks and new patterns of behaviour. Existing entities struggle to change and so are superseded by newcomers whose key distinguishing feature is their ability to adapt. In the future, we must understand adaptability better. There are three factors that test adaptability by testing the status quo:

> **Impotent Forces** Under the attack of these forces, the target does not need to change to survive. Such forces are, by nature, ineffective; they do not possess the potency to represent a threat. Yet, they often appear potent and, so, many react to them and waste themselves. In history, many emperors have taken their armies to battle not realising they were impotent against a far superior force. The Romans repeatedly defeated such impotent forces in building their empire.
>
> **Important Forces** The threat of these forces is potent, and when under assault from such a force the target needs to adapt to survive. Having swept aside forces that turned out to be impotent in the face of his army, Hitler faced an important force in the shape of the British.
>
> **Shocking Forces** Such forces transform the very situation and the target becomes irrelevant. The surviving entities are sufficiently different from the previous ones to survive and thrive in the new situation. In Vietnam, in Mogadishu, in the early days of the second Iraq War the Americans faced forces that shocked them. They found themselves unprepared for the tactics of the enemy.

Winners lose when they fail to understand which of the above forces they are facing and fail to respond appropriately. The nature of the challenge therefore is to adapt with a force and speed appropriate to the shift in the environment. Strategies that survive will instil critical capabilities into their entities and create the Intelligent

Adaptive System we explored earlier. In order of ascending superiority, the choices of capabilities will be as follows:

Retaliation Capability This strategy instils retaliatory behaviour into the entity as a 'natural' response. An institution (team, community, corporation or government) following this strategy is naturally inclined to retaliate in the face of attack, believing that if it follows only a defensive strategy, the attack may never end. The strategy involves the sending of a message to deter further attack, the strength of the retaliation has the potential to deter strongly or, under certain circumstances, raises the stakes until the situation escalates and abuse is required to sustain position.

Abusive Capability This strategy is characterised by a willingness to abuse the position of power in order to maintain a situation or state of affairs. The forms vary and include predatory competition; changes to or mis-interpretation of laws to prevent others participating or to justify abusive strategies, and the use of position to force boycotting and intimidation of new entrants. Such an entity is naturally inclined to abuse its power and to justify to itself the validity of its methods. As we have already said, when a system is no longer fit, its position is not sustainable without an abuse of power. Abuse of power is of course not sustainable if there is a large bank of the abused who are willing to do whatever it takes to overthrow the abusers.

Flexibility This strategy is characterised by the ability to change as circumstances change. An institution following this strategy is naturally inclined to be flexible in the face of changes in its environment. It will have the potential to avoid losing ground by shifting its own position, thus avoiding the abusive strategies that most ego-driven entities feel are necessary. However, athough flexibility is a key ingredient in survival, it leads to a lack of trustworthiness in the absence of purpose, or widely accepted purpose.

Fluidity This strategy requires the ability to change in a smooth manner so that the organisation is always refining its position. An institution with this characteristic never embraces a fixed position. Fluidity is an extension of a flexible strategy. The key difference is the absence of a position that needs to be changed substantially.

Revolutionary Capability This strategy requires the instilling of the ability to revolt to trigger large-scale change. An institution with this capability is inclined to challenge and overthrow its system and embrace another more appropriate one. It is prepared to suffer the significant transitional losses of destroying existing leaders and their ways. The 20th-century revolutions in Russia, Mexico and China raised the spectre for future leaders that their populations were instilled with a revolutionary potential.

Evolutionary Capability This strategy instils the ability to evolve. An institution with this capability is naturally inclined to find the next form and allow itself to change into that form. The key difference from the revolutionary capability is that the cost of transition is lower. Ultimately, the resulting entity may be the same. The challenge is to be open to the enormity of the potential change. Nature provides the most interesting parallels for this form of strategy: the creature that crawled had no conceivable conception of its ability to walk, and that creature in turn had no conceivable conception of its ability to fly. However, the potential for each one was present in the previous one.

The biggest threat to the successful is the enshrining of their success as an ideology. The critical realisation for us is to see that, given the enormous number of entities, levers and potential movements in these entities at any given time, it is not possible to create strategies continually that respond. As we explored in some detail in the previous chapter in our discussion on Intelligent Adaptive Systems, the aim should be to create a system that succeeds. The role of the strategist is therefore to build the system such that it is fit for survival. This involves the building of capabilities in the system. As a systems engineer, the strategist will need to specify the system, design it, mastermind its creation, deploy it, monitor it, refine it, destroy it and rebuild it.

Future strategic investigation will need to focus on the role of the Master Strategist as someone who creates evolving systems.

SEVEN: THE ROLE OF MANKIND

The human species is eroding the assets of the planet – its land, water, minerals, peoples, animals, plants and air – but has no adequate strategies for replacement. According to one view, Mankind is a pestilence on the land, although according to another, despite imbalances, Mankind is the transforming agent of base materials into a higher form and so the overall effect is positive. Such issues cannot be addressed using existing methods of strategy analysis. Increasingly, we need to pursue a more sophisticated line of enquiry to find the answers to such fundamental questions as:

- Is it possible to create a civilisation that generates peace, prosperity and freedom for the whole of humanity as well as other species?
- Is it possible to create nations that share with each other their physical and intellectual assets and still renew these assets?
- Is it possible to create organisations that maximise the

opportunities and development of those that participate in them?

• Is it possible to create individuals who are balanced in their dealings with themselves, their loved ones and others?

A number of studies have attempted to calculate the maximum population that could be supported by our planet. If the people of earth lived at the affluence level of the US with all the associated freedoms and with few restrictions on commerce, pollution, land use and personal behaviour, the planet could sustain 0.5 billion people. If we add some restrictions to commerce, pollution, land use and behaviour by curtailing the 'open' economy, the planet could sustain 2 billion people.[2] If we add massive recycling, restrictions on driving cars by rationing fuel, restrict transport even of food, prohibit the cutting of trees, limit the burning of fossil fuels, limit the areas of open spaces even for renewable energy power plants in order to preserve natural areas for atmospheric oxygen generation and food growing and completely saturate roof tops and parking lots for solar energy production, we can support 4 billion at the American affluence level. If we are willing to accept that only people in the US and Europe should stay at their current level of affluence and everyone else must live at the current prosperity level of Mexico, Earth could support 6 billion people. If everyone lived at Mexico's current prosperity level, we could support 20 billion. If everyone lived at the current 'prosperity' level of Northwest Africa, we could support 40 billion people.[3]

So, one possibility is that, given the way we live today, in the future there may be no such thing as a higher human law, only the rule of survival based on weight of numbers. As the population grows, our liberties, grand values and rights may have to take a back seat to the more basic struggle of early humans: survival.

The most critical long-term strategic thinking will need to focus on strategies for whole systems, such as the ecosystem. We know already that wealth generation systems without wealth distribution systems do not lead to sustainable models for society: the 20th-century worker revolutions of Russia and China were fuelled by these inequalities. Similarly, strategy for the planet will also need to focus on the planet's 'system' and the interaction with and between other systems, such as political, trade and economic systems.

To develop strategies for such systems and the interactions between them, we will need to identify both the systems and the nature of the interactions. There are many ways to classify these systems. One way is to categorise them as five hierarchical systems. Each level in the hierarchy has intervention points that provide ways for the Master Strategist to influence the system. Although there are many bases for exploring such a huge topic, we will conduct our exploration from the perspective of Mankind.

So, the systems and the connection between systems comes from the following:

- The basis of the overall system is the Individual. Common interests lead Individuals to form Cells.
- The next level is the Cell. The Cell is an organisational unit of Individuals. Interdependence leads Cells to coalesce to form a People.
- The next level is People. People are communities of Cells. Mutual need, in particular trade, leads Peoples to form Alliances.
- The next level is Alliances. Alliances are coalitions and

communities of interests and ideas. Winning, and losing, lead Alliances to become civilisations.

- The final level, from Mankind's perspective, is Civilisation. Civilisations are the dominant force of a time that reach an equilibrium that enables the co-existence of others whilst asserting their own way.

Depending on the level at which he operates, the strategist has either five points, or five roles, which enable him to intervene to develop the system:

1   *Person(al) Development* The aim is to develop fit individuals, who are fit to adapt and, therefore, fit to survive.

2   *Organisation Development* The aim is to develop a fit organisation.

3   *Factor Development* The aim is to develop communities and the resources that enable them to live in balance with the environment.

4   *Beliefs and Behaviour Development* The aim is to develop cooperative mutually beneficial alliances between communities.

5   *Interconnectedness Development* The aim is to develop the civilisation so that it can exist within the total system.

When strategies focus on development, we add value to the whole. As such, every part of the system has a contribution to make, as does each individual, as the basic unit of the whole. Each unit can be strategic. The history of Man since he evolved from being merely a hunter, has been to form Man-centric structures that place him in direct conflict with the environment. As technology has advanced, Man has become more proficient at shaping the environment to suit his needs.

This has taken the form of huge metropolises, oil rigs, airports and deforestation projects. Over many millennia, this strategy results in what became known in the late 20th century as 'unsustainable development'.

Sustainable development requires strategies that advance the system by which we live on the planet. It requires Man to develop strategies to develop more sustainable ways of living (people or person[al] development), organising (organisational development), resourcing (factor development), cooperating (beliefs and behaviour development) and being (inter-connectedness development).

THE AGENDA FOR BREAKING THE LIMITATIONS OF STRATEGY

When each of the above strategic paths has been explored by pioneering strategists, we will arrive at new strategic principles, frameworks, techniques and actions. These will soon become fads, and then we will need to begin again. To do this, we will need a calibre of strategist capable of creating new techniques, new approaches and new states of existence to enable people and institutions to be at peace, to prosper and to be free.

To break through our current limitations, we need to achieve continuity, which will prevent us becoming over-dependent on outdated strategies. This renewal capability will require continuous thinking, continuous change and continuous being. We need continuous development of: our thinking so that we can develop strategies of the type described in this section, continuous change so that we do not become static and inflexible in the face of the enormous changes facing us and continuous development of the civilisation of human beings so that we live in a more sustainable way.

There are no breakthroughs in thinking that are permanent, there is no change that is lasting and there is no state that can last forever. The agenda for the Master Strategist is to transform individuals, transform institutions and transform relationships. In the next chapter, we will examine what it takes to create such strategists.

6

CREATING MASTERY

'Strategists are produced by overcoming barriers. The level at which they play is determined by opportunity. Opportunity may arise or can be created by oneself or by institutions. To maximise the chance of transforming talent into mastery, opportunity must be institutionalised. Every hurdle must be put in the way of this talent to enable testing, elimination and refinement.'

The Book of Power, Purpose and Principle

THE NEED TO CREATE MASTERY

In this chapter we will lay out the agenda for addressing the many challenges posed in this book:

- Can we achieve peace, prosperity and freedom through our existing institutions?
- Can we address the challenges we face without the existence of a broad and deep strategic talent pool?
- Can a strategic talent pool be created or can it only be selected?
- What are the conditions under which more strategic talent emerges?
- What is the role of leaders in creating the institutions and the talent required to seize the enormous

opportunities and combat the threats?
- What is the role of the individual in creating mastery?
- Can the process of creating mastery be speeded up?

How many more wars before we learn peace? How many more feudal systems of enterprise before we learn prosperity? How many more inequitable regimes before we learn to honour liberty? We do not appear to be able to learn fast enough from our experiences and events are changing faster and faster. These changes are phenomenal because of the potential scale and nature of their impact, which can be discontinuous, multiple and comprise interconnected causes-and-effects. These changes are reshaping the environment we live in today, and as a result a gap is being created between the nature of the challenge and our capability. With time, the gap is widening. As the gap widens, we are becoming less and less fit to close the gap.

This situation places a heavy burden on leaders and individuals to assess, form a point of view and to participate in change. We must assess whether our existing institutions can create adequate responses to address these phenomenal issues and, if not, whether our leaders can (re)invent them. We must also assess whether our strategists can mastermind our response to these issues and, if not, whether our leaders can develop this capability. We must assess, too, whether we as individuals can cope with these issues and, if not, whether we can develop our own capabilities.

What we are experiencing is profound because it represents the biggest challenge to our existing civilisation. Unfortuantely, we do not have either the analytic tools or the 'super-consciousness' in efficient quantity to understand the impact of this challenge.

We find ourselves today more connected, more knowledgeable, more prosperous, more resourceful, and therefore more powerful, than ever before. With all this power, we have circled back to the need for survival and security. The quality of our strategies will determine the outcome. Unfortunately, our existing strategies – in areas as fundamental as international relations, trade, aid, commerce, national affairs, communal relations, personal relationships – are, once again, creating situations and systems that cannot survive.

The appropriate response to such phenomenal change needs to be discontinuous, multiple and interconnected. This will lead to the creation of a new civilisation. The world has had bloody transitions to new civilisations before. So, in some ways this is no different from the eras of our past. Our challenge is to see if we can make this move without wasting too much of what we have.

THE AGENDA FOR MASTERY

In mastering this change, there is an institutional component and a personal one. These challenges will not be met without fundamental changes in nine key areas:

1   Our world view
2   The basis of our strategies
3   The language and concepts we use
4   The institutions that exercise strategy
5   The characteristics and qualities of our leaders
6   Our methods and techniques
7   The patterns of our interaction with each other
8   The willingness of strategists to pursue a rigorous path of development
9   Our ability to move beyond strategy

New World View

We fall into two categories: those that see the need for a fundamental shift and those that do not. The latter hide their fear of change by justifying why the existing institutions, leaders and strategists and their methods and techniques are adequate. They claim that we are already making the necessary changes and their position relies on others believing them. Without this belief we are ready to change. Fear, combined with the illusion of continuity, drugs our sensibilities and subdues our deepest instincts. Delusions of safety need to be shattered to force us into action. A new world view needs to be shaped by Master Strategists combining the analytic and the intuitive. This combination will enable patterns to be formed from the base data and new potential paths to be identified. Examples of patterns derived from the elements already present include a range of new possibilities for the first two decades of the 21st century:

- The assassination of a key political leader, who could be American, British or Russian, given the anti-establishment forces present in or outside each of these countries.
- The embroiling of the US in a crisis of leadership in one of its less stable allies, for example Pakistan, because of the support given to the US by the Pakistani leader during the war in Afghanistan following 9/11 and the strong anti-American sentiments of his countrymen.
- The collapse of one of the BRICs governments, given their meteoric economic growth, shaking the international growth story.
- The collapse of the US currency, mirroring the way that sterling went following the decline of Britain as a Superpower after the Second World War, as a result of

continuing doubts about US economic and foreign policy.

- The collapse of one of the major oil states, triggering an oil crisis and international conflict.
- US failure of the type that occurred at Mogadishu in 1993, heralding the fact that the US is increasingly fallible.
- A crisis of confidence for key US corporations and investors, following the continuation of financial and regulatory investigations, who turn to US markets as a result.
- Sabotage of vital financial and communication networks by enemies of globalisation and by the al-Qaeda network.
- Conflict between the US and the US-established Iraqi regime as a result of the latter pursuing non-US friendly policies both in the country and the region.
- The US feeling compelled to 'deal with' Iran's nuclear sites.
- The debilitating impact of a major health scare, or acceleration of AIDs, on a part of the world so that it becomes an international no-go zone.
- A major oil-leak, nuclear explosion or ozone-destroying event through accident, neglect or intent, so that there is a devastating impact on our environment, marking a step-change in the acceleration of the decline of the fitness of our planet to sustain life.

The formulation of compelling world views that both capture the imagination of the mass audience and enable a Master Strategist to capture the moment is a difficult task. It requires the right candidates to 'flower' under the right conditions. We should not expect that only benevolent Master

Strategists will arise. At various points in history, the circumstances have been, and will continue to be right for an emperor, a Master Strategist, to emerge. One interpretation of history is that Alexander, Genghis Khan, Attila, Tokugawa Ieyasu and Hitler all arose when the circumstances were right for them to flower and prevail. Lord Tokugawa Ieyasu, the Japanese Shogun, seized power at the end of breakthroughs by two great generals – Lord Hideyoshi and Lord Nobunaga, who had conducted bloody battles of unification across Japan – to establish a family empire that lasted for 264 years. Let us take one interpretation of the history of the times to illustrate what could be the flowering conditions in the early 21st century. The conditions that illustrate the concept are as follows:

- The first condition would be the demonstration of the ability to strike at the heart of the sole and undisputed Superpower, America. This was demonstrated by the small force of revolutionaries who toppled the 'Twin Towers' in New York on 11 September 2001.
- The next condition would be the evidence that such acts had the potential support of a large part of the Islamic world because they had a common enemy. This support would have been shown to exist in the heart of the Superpower itself, in its allies' lands, in the Middle East and in South East Asia.
- America retaliated against its enemies in Afghanistan and won popular international support. It stood on the brink of uniting the world for a greater purpose: to rid the world of terror. However, because of the way that it conducted its campaign against its next target, Iraq, which was questioned by its allies and enemies alike, America lost the moment to lead the world. This was the next condition.

- A supporting condition would be evidence that America's moral standing was questioned more widely. This would be achieved not only through a series of media trials all over the world, but also through actual trials in America that questioned American conduct. America would have appeared to be willing to reinterpret its own laws regarding detention as well as the rights of its own citizens, and to challenge and contravene commonly accepted international principles.

- The next condition would be to show others the way to resist might. The resistance in Iraq showed the way. It became clear that there was a process of diversion, decoy and deception that could confuse and frustrate a Superpower.

- Factions of the Iraqi resistance conducted bombings, kidnappings, ransoms, tortures, beheadings and inflicted serious collateral damage on civilians. This not only alienated the American allies that had spoken against America but also their own potential supporters. So, whereas the first wave of attackers against America showed what works when striking at an enemy, the next wave showed what does not work. They had demonstrated how to waste the opportunity to unite a large proportion of the Islamic world. This failure was an important lesson for those that might come next.

- Iran was emerging as the new Middle East Superpower. It had a rich ancient Persian history of military campaigns, culture, arts and sciences. In modern times, Iran had a massive land mass, a substantial population, a nuclear programme and, perhaps, most important of all, oil. It presented a formidable potential force. Its oil attracted China, the rising Superpower, to develop trading relations and to become a potential future barrier to pre-emptive US action. This was the final major condition: the creation of a formidable and relatively secure force in the Middle East.

Although in the early 2000s America had the potential to be the greatest force for 'good' in the world, its motives came frequently under question, thereby undermining its ability to realise this. It had strengths that far outweighed others' and made it a potent force. The positive factors in America's favour included the strength and size of its capital markets, its predominant corporations, its military capability, its innovation and scientific leadership, its extraordinarily creative and imaginative media industry and the optimistic and the generally positive nature of its people. These positive factors could lead to a 'domino-effect' of peace and liberty across the Middle East and then the rest of the world.

Given the above 'flowering' conditions, the first two decades of the 21st century would present one of the great opportunities for an 'emperor' to emerge. Such an emperor could be an American. However, the scenario with the potential to shake the world would be the rise of such an emperor from the Islamic world. In reaction, America would become more hardline. This hardening would be directed not just at its enemies, but also against economic rivals such as China. In reaction, China would also become more hardline. In the midst of this hardening of stances, the relevance of Europe would be challenged.

Master Strategy would be required either to prevent the circumstances from continuing to foster the growth and rise of such an emperor or to turn such an emperor into a benevolent force.

The ancient books of the great religions were venerated for their wisdom. It is a time for great wisdom once again. Many compelling world views are possible, the moment can be captured and new paths can be created because the elements required for all paths are always present. It takes both introspection and extrospection to find these paths. A new basis of strategy is required to take the high ground of a powerful, purposeful and principled position.

The New Basis of Strategy: Power, Purpose and Principle

Powerful forces can shape people's strategies for all aspects of their lives. In the 20th century, three of these forces were focus on personal wealth; the cult of the leader, which resulted in the concentration of power; and the increasing mass media propagation of simplistic formulae for success. As a consequence, people have tended to pursue a narrow definition of power based on self-interested purpose and circumstantial principles. In the 21st century, this cannot be changed without a fundamental change to our collective personal psyches.

If we are to achieve 'good', strategists will need to follow principles such as the Three Laws of Strategy, namely:

1   To rise above the conflicting bodies and identify a higher common position.
2   To determine how to take whole and thereby minimise waste and destruction.
3   To see an event as belonging within a flow of events and so to react within the context of the flow not just the event.

The implications are wide ranging. Traditionally, power is defined as the enforcing of our will on others. Purpose, in this context, is usually about gaining more power and more wealth, while principles are usually a combination of social, cultural and religious constructs that are conveniently dismissed when it comes to seeking power and wealth. When the agenda for leaders change to one that is focused on peace, prosperity and freedom, the very definition of these terms change:

- Power equals the enhancement of freedoms, as long as there is no conflict with purpose and principles.
- Purpose equals the pursuit of that which is required to achieve peace, prosperity and freedom in a manner fit for the circumstances, as long as there is no conflict with power and principles.
- Principle equals the pursuit of truth, and this has no limits.

The strategies that will result from these definitions have the potential to transform our lives and lead us to a new and more positive era. Examples of the directions we may take to break our prevailing pattern include the following scenarios.

- The rise of more and more 'mature' women (and more men willing to acknowledge and value their 'feminine' attributes) to substantial positions of leadership, resulting in a more compassionate and considered approach to conflict and competition
- The resolution of border conflicts and territorial unrest through agreement on a higher aim for the land and its people. In the early 21st century this would focus on India and Pakistan, China, Taiwan and Tibet, Israel and Palestine, Russia and Chechnya.
- The alleviation of the burdens of structurally flawed countries. These countries are structurally flawed because of the harshness of the natural environment, the

abuse of people by their leaders and the absence of
formal institutions. In the early 21st century this
condition afflicted many of the African and some of the
Latin American nations.

- The general acceptance of an agreement of common
  principles between the Islamic and non-Islamic world,
  backed by the flow of trade, people and know-how.
- The ending of divides. This would be fuelled by the rise
  of corporations that lead in their communities. Such
  corporations would use their resources to create wealth
  for themselves and their communities and also to
  address fundamental issues. In the early 21st century,
  this would result in a pharmaceutical sector that
  supported health education, medication and services to
  those on the poorer side of the health divide as part of
  their portfolio of activities. Similarly, technology
  companies would eradicate the digital divide,
  educational institutions the education divide and power
  generators the energy divide. Corporate leaders would
  no longer define their role as being concerned only with
  short-term wealth generation and instead consider
  themselves to be leaders laying the foundations for long-
  term wealth generation.
- The renewal of the earth's environment and resources.
  Breakthroughs would be required in the areas of
  biotechnology and genetics, nanotechnology and
  alternative mass energy sources. Such breakthroughs
  would enable us to create alternative materials,
  alternative ways of healing and alternatives to oil and
  gas. Three ingredients would be applied: a gratis capital
  expenditure of enormous size, a compelling race similar
  in magnitude to that conducted by US President
  Kennedy against the Soviet Union to put a man on the

moon, and competitive-collaborative efforts between scientists and engineers.

- The unlocking of human potential based on rethinking the structure, content and methods of education. In the early part of the 21st century, we have the ability to make a radical break with the learning methods of the recent past and pursue a new path. This new path would use the richness of Man's history, our accumulated knowledge, methods and techniques to create new educational establishments. The new path would seek to unlock human potential rather than prepare us for the shallow tests of the prevailing education system.

- The creation of the World Peace Foundation. Given the 21st century's lack of global leadership on peace, prosperity and freedom, an institute would be created that brought together the strands of thought laid out in this book, and others of its type, to address the fundamental issues and opportunities in the world. If the location were to be China's Xizang, Tibet, it would create the most powerful and unique force for good in the world. The Chinese government would then become the catalyst responsible for galvanising the world to re-focus on fundamental issues.

These are not formulae, nor are they the limits of the agenda we need to create. Strategy needs to set us free, not to bind us to our limitations.

New Language and Concepts

We know that our language forms our reality. The language we use externally (spoken) and internally (thought and dreamt) provides meaning to our external experiences (events and relationships) and our internal ones (our emotions and thoughts).

We have allowed the language of military affairs to govern the language of strategy and relationships. The language of military strategy is indeed powerful and useful in examining strategy, but its overwhelming use has biased our view of how strategy should be conducted. This means that the language of strategy, in all tongues, conveys rivalry, division and winning. We talk of enemies and rivals, competition, share, human resource and competence.

Our ideas need to be changed through new language that only uses this predominantly conflict-based language when it truly means it. As a result of our new language (and in due course our actions) we will recognise others as participants rather than enemies or rivals, as we too often do now. We will also focus on the expansion of possibilities rather than always on competition, and will seek growth rather than just market share. We will develop people's potential rather than manage human resources, and will talk more about character, values and potential than competence.

We need to develop a new lexicon drawing on a wide array of fields to create new ideas. Our language, and therefore our strategies, will be coloured and textured, but not limited, by:

- The language of Chaos Theory
- The language of Intelligent Adaptive Systems Theory
- The language of the physical, biological and natural sciences
- The language of peace and compassion
- The language of the pursuit of awareness
- The language of technology, engineering and architecture, design and the arts

We will have succeeded when we have created a language that reflects the richness of our existence. The resulting diversity and openness to ideas will enable strategists to change minds.

New Institutions

Governments govern, armies wage war, schools teach, surgeons cut and corporations profit. The world we live in is a reflection, in part, of the institutions that we have established. The results we get should be of no surprise to us, given the institutions that we have established. If we wish to have leadership, peace, development, healing and sharing we need to change the institutions that produce today's results. This will require some of our existing institutions to be replaced, some to be reformed, as well as some new ones to be added.

One of the fundamental transformations required is the establishment of additional and more powerful institutions of peace. We have dedicated an enormous amount of our energy to winning war. We have institutionalised this learning in various institutions of war, such as the army, navy and air force. Specialised institutions and elite forces capable of addressing particular situations have been created. Secret services and government departments have dedicated themselves to studying the various ways in which to win wars. We have national academies to train our state warriors, private academies for training armies of mercenaries and university courses to study war. We have created technologies that enable us to wage war more effectively. We have created companies that specialise in researching, developing and manufacturing the technologies and weapons of war. In addition, trading organisations and mechanisms exist to generate wealth for us from trading weapons with our allies and arming our enemies.

In short, we have invested heavily in the institutions that make us effective at conducting war. Given our current stage of development, much of this has been highly necessary. The best of these institutions have established new standards in human discipline and endurance. The countless accounts of acts of courage and selfless endeavour demonstrate the calibre of the men and women in these institutions.

The institutions of peace were created following the major wars of the 20th century. The UN, one of these institutions, was established to promote peace and co-operation in the world using peacekeeping troops drawn from member countries when required. In 1948, the UN Universal Declaration of Human Rights spoke of all men being born free and equal in dignity and rights. Such institutions were intended to establish international order and be forums for united action. However, most are constrained by mandate, finances, veto, bureaucracy and talent. In short, we have not made anywhere near the investment required to make us effective at conducting peace. Perversely, our investment in the institutions of war is valuable, as much of this investment will also help us more directly address peace. To achieve this we need to establish:

- A land, sea and air peace corps to engage others in peace
- Government departments and independent groups dedicated to studying the ways in which to win peace
- University courses to study types and methods for establishing peace
- Companies that specialise in researching, develop-menting and manufacturing the technologies and techniques that will enable us to create peace
- Trading organisations and mechanisms to generate wealth for ourselves, our allies and our enemies, which in turn will create security

- Public and private academies for training people in more peaceful ways

The establishment of such institutions will require a transformation of our approach to international relations, government, study and education, and action. They will need the mandate to attract capital, talent and intellectual property. The resulting revolution has the potential to cause enormous unrest since so many of our existing institutions will feel threatened.

We will not succeed in one attempt. The execution of these changes can be split into six phases. Firstly, the launch, when leaders will need to win the hearts and minds of their people and launch an enormous coordinated effort to establish the institutions of peace. Next, the management of conflict, as a successful launch will cause a shift in resources, and therefore power, from the prevailing institutions of war to those of peace. Rehabilitation will follow as successful launches will require those stuck in the war paradigm to be rehabilitated and unsuccessful launches will require a fight to re-launch. Re-balancing will be the next phase, because leaders will have gone too far and may have weakened their armies of war too much and too soon in a world that may well still need powerful forces of war. Execution follows with the engagement of peace corps and the other institutions in addressing the issues that normally lead to war. This will enable the capability to be tested and built. Finally, the effort to maintain perpetual peace, since breaking the cycle of war will result in the transformation of international, national, communal and personal relations and this will be difficult to maintain.

Do we have the leaders to forge such an age?

In addition to the institutions of peace described above, our educational institutions, industrial zones, companies and communities will also need to be reformed, augmented or replaced. We will need to invest in the creation of the following institutions:

Development Academies The purpose of these will be to unlock human potential. This would require us to take from the richness of the world's history and teach our children how to be peaceful, prosperous and free. We would need to include technical training, methods and techniques, knowledge of the disciplines and specialisation. The content would include the sciences, arts and meditation to develop physical, emotional and mental awareness.

Innovation and Development Valleys and Hubs The purpose of these hubs would be to concentrate our wealth creation in specific areas within a country, to maximise the chance of making breakthroughs, of attracting talent and capital and of creating commercial enterprises. These hubs would then spread capability and prosperity nationally and internationally.

Re-Corporate Institutions Our corporations have generally embraced a narrow definition of their role in society. This definition embraces two stakeholders at the expense of others: the shareholder and the management. This model is therefore inherently an unstable one and can only survive through the abuse of the rights of other interest groups. The companies of the future will wield their resources to create wealth in a way that is more appropriate. It will be more appropriate because it will also address fundamental issues within their chosen domain. Business missions and practices would include 'everyday low prices', 'solving the health issues of the world' and 'enhancing people's lives through technology'. However, companies would have to mean it and carry it out. Today, these statements are often only marketing slogans, although those that truly mean it have done enormously well for the period in which they meant it. Corporate leaders will need to become leaders in their societies rather than just in their stock market categories if they are to avoid being hated, sued and imprisoned.

Virtual Communities As our world becomes more open, transparent and interconnected, we will increasingly be faced with virtual communities of, for example, professionals, entrepreneurs, traders, terrorists and movie makers. We will need to understand this phenomenon and learn to use the means by which such communities form so that we can make a step-change in the way we conduct peace, education, business and personal affairs.

Again, the same question applies: do we have the leaders to forge such an age?

New Characteristics and Qualities: Forging Leaders

The character and qualities of the strategist and of the entity for which the strategies are developed are two of the key opening determinants in any situation. The development of these qualities is critical to the ability to deal with situations.

Most of our development lore focuses on personal qualities. This has, to a limited extent, provided useful development plans. Most of these focus on the development of techniques, such as presentation, negotiation, brainstorming and the reading of body language. To develop a new cadre of strategic professionals, we will need to focus on a wider and deeper set of qualities that go to the core of strategic presence of mind, body and spirit.

The development of the strategist will involve developing the ability to:

Form View This will require instilling the ability to create techniques, analyse, remain focused, clear noise, rely on instinct, see patterns, imagine possibilities, make leaps in thinking, see the detail as well as the whole, draw potential paths, see nodal points and develop stories that both capture people's imagination and illustrate possibilities.

Take positions This will require instilling the ability both to create and dissolve positions, as well as the ability to reposition in a continuous manner or in a step-change manner, if so required.

Exercise Influence This will require being able to work with the minds of others, dealing with cause-and-effect, unlimiting limited assets, controlling time, acting in an inter-connected manner, developing continuous and natural strategies and dealing with the bigger issues of power, purpose and principle.

The characteristics and qualities of the strategist and the entity for which we strategise are similar. There are three qualities that describe the strategic state of both. The first is being capable, the ability to deal with whatever comes up. The second is readiness. This state encapsulates alertness, being beyond surprise and being ready to act. The third is spontaneity. This state encapsulates sensitivity, intuition and a speed of reaction beyond the need to mentally process the situation.

The aim is to develop character and qualities that will facilitate the move from developing strategy to being in a strategic state.

New Methods and Techniques

Our methods and techniques determine our response. As

discussed in Chapter two, our existing methods and techniques for strategy development are flawed in many important ways. Hence, the quality of our response has become more and more inadequate, particularly given the challenges we now face.

The ways we conduct strategy need to be broadened to include competition, disruption, domination, inclusion and aspiration. For each of these ways, methods and techniques need to be introduced that enable more effective:

Competition This involves methods and techniques to beat the mind of the rival.

Disruption This involves methods and techniques that cause a change to the course, functioning or nature of the enemy's system, akin to infecting the enemy with a virus.

Domination This involves methods and techniques to create followership amongst rivals by creating uneven power in relationships.

Inclusion This involves methods and techniques that lead to collaboration, so that the partners can win together.

Aspiration This involves methods and techniques that redefine the prevailing realities by redefining the beliefs and aspirations of participants.

The methods and techniques described in this work are also a crutch. The more we rely on them the less relevant they will become. Breakthroughs are required to find new ways of conducting strategy. Once popularised, these methods will also become a crutch and will need to be replaced.

If we are successful, we will move beyond strategies that limit our view and bias our response. The aim is to develop and apply methods and techniques that will enable us to address successfully the fundamental issues facing us, whatever these issues may be.

New Patterns of Interaction

As previously discussed, our history leads us to predictable patterns of behaviour: over-analytic, limited in scope, extrapolation based on past trends and rational argument hiding fear and greed. The result is that our leaders have a tendency to wage a limited war for the mind and a prolonged war for the 'body', the land.

If we are to advance, new patterns of interaction are required to unlock the potential value now evident to us. To achieve this we will need to change the pattern of our interaction and therefore, our relationship with our enemies, our allies, our leaders, our employers, our communities, our families and ourselves. Such new patterns would be based on the following new behaviours:

The Seeking of Cause This new pattern of behaviour would require us to seek a cause for the outcomes and situations we find ourselves in. It would require us to stop blaming chance and stop demonising the enemy. Ultimately, we would see the role that we played both in the things that go well for us and in those that do not go so well.

The Engineering of Causes-and-Effects In the future, a well-developed strategy of interconnectedness will help us to better understand the impact we have on the world. We would use causes such as triggers, thoughts, actions, spontaneous events and natural laws. We would also create different types of effects, such as the multiplier effect, the domino-effect, programmed effects, spontaneous effects and reactions.

The Transformation of the Value of Resources We have come to expect that the thing to do to resources is to manage them, whereas in the future we will need to embrace the principle that the thing to do with resources is to transform their value. This will stop the unnecessary fights for limited resources. Our energy will instead be focused on magnifying the impact of our resources, stretching them, applying them more intensely, enhancing their ingenuity, functionality, composition and organisation.

The Creation of More Time This is necessary so we can resolve our issues and unlock our opportunities. Losing time creates anxieties and fears that lead us to act in more destructive ways. Wasting time leads to lost time. So, the idea is to create time and make the maximum use of it. If we are successful, time will no longer be quite the limiting factor that we perceive it to be today.

The distinguishing feature of how we interact with each other will be the fact that we act in the light of our belief in the truth and value of our interconnectedness, our diversity and our potential. This will require counter-cultural behaviour. For example, the powerful will need to forgo power; the military will need to embrace the absence of war; CEOs will need to forgo short-term profit; and enemies will need to become compassionate. None of this is possible without the parallel development of mature individuals as strategists and citizens.

New Development Path

Our existing methods are producing inadequate strategists. Inadequate because, unable to deal with myriad forces facing them, they create strategies that are unfit for purpose. In addition, they are mostly not strategists, they are analysts, experts or merely people in positions of power.

'Maturity' is required to be a strategist. This maturity requires awareness which, in turn, comes from experience. No amount of purely intellectual effort can compensate for combining both intellectual and sensory experience. We know that the great leaders of history all had an intensity of experience that prepared them for greatness: Genghis Khan's hardships in youth, Alexander's exposure to power and intrigue, and Mao's hunted existence and exposure to the crushed proletariat all prepared them for greatness. Growing up in a safe, comfortable and unchallenging environment is unlikely to prepare us for great strategic thinking or leadership. This is not to say that environment is the only determining factor or that we should create a punitive environment as a matter of course. However, if we seek to develop men and women of great courage, capability and character they will need to experience an environment that fosters this. It is because they recognise the importance of a controlled environment in producing people of a certain type that the army takes control of people's lives. So, the challenge for the educators and the individual is to determine what environment they are prepared to create to engineer successful strategists.

The strategist will need to develop a deep awareness of his own inside world as well as the outside world. This is one of the most difficult hurdles for most strategists, as we have been trained to avoid introspection. Our education system, work environment, entertainment mode and leisure time all focus on doing things. Introspection requires the absence of doing, a state we feel uncomfortable with. The Christian practice of monastic silence, the Chinese practice of t'ai chi and meditation, the Japanese practice of Zen meditation and the Indian practice of yoga and meditation all point us in these directions. But we cannot reach these states intellectually. We have to do things that instil an inner stillness.

An effective world view needs to consist of awareness of our physical dimension, our emotions, our deeper mind, the objects of our mind and the interaction between these elements. The objects of our enquiry need to be wide ranging and so require strategists to have an understanding of topics as diverse as people, money, science and technology, the environment and energy. This presents us with another problem. Our leaders are either unable or unwilling to invest the time to develop the understanding required to formulate great strategy. They are not required to know everything, but they do need to be able to judge and decide.

The function of strategy is to deliver a result. Maturity is the intrinsic quality that will distinguish great results from not so great ones. This maturity comes from possessing four qualities: being in the flow of data and information; being knowledge-able; being insightful; and being foresightful. The process that enables us to become foresightful involves building three capabilities: analysis, experience and wisdom. This path is not one that many will choose to follow. And so, strategists are rarely engineered or nurtured. Strategists develop their innate potential in response to stimuli.

Given the enormous challenges facing us, the real task for leaders is to engineer the creation of mature strategists, what I have referred to in this book as Master Strategists. To engineer this mastery we must create the conditions that create it.

BEING IN THE INFORMATION FLOW

The Master Strategist will be connected to the flow of information. Our jobs place us in a flow of information. Some jobs place us in more of the flow of information than others. The secret services are in a unique flow of information regarding politics and political figures, investment bankers are in a unique flow of information regarding their clients' intentions as regards mergers and acquisitions; research pharmacists are in a unique flow of information regarding the adverse impact of new medication. So, what flow of information does a strategist need to be in to be effective?

In today's world, the flow of data and information required by the strategist can be split into that required for the internal and external levers that he must pull to execute strategy. The information flow regarding internal levers includes an organisation's leaders; its population of people; its physical assets; its capital; its information and intellectual assets; and its belief system, code, culture or way of doing things. The information flow regarding external levers includes knowledge of all the above for other relevant entities; the physical terrain; the information terrain; the political, regulatory and legal terrain; the military and security terrain; the cultural terrain resulting from the interconnection of subcultures that define a pattern of human intercourse; the financial systems' terrain resulting from the composite of credit, payments and capital markets.

The strategist will need data in its 'raw' form (for example, statistics), as well as in a more processed form (information) so that he can be in touch with the 'realities' of the world.

BEING KNOWLEDGEABLE

Master Strategists will be people of their time with a keen understanding of the issues (such as the types of shaping phenomena described in the opening chapter), and the content relevant to their world (such as money, science and technology and physical force).

Let us examine one of the challenges for a strategist by looking briefly at the transforming role that technology will increasingly play in our world. In the 21st century, Man is set to see:

- The transformation of natural matter – materials

and organisms – into artificial matter using nano-technology.

- The transformation of programmed machines into intelligent learning machines using artificial intelligence software and hardware.
- The transformation of chemical medicines into individualised biological and gene specific solutions through biotechnology and genetics.
- The transformation of oil-based energy into all manner of alternative natural and synthetic energy.
- The transformation of the microcosm of our lives through the application of solutions that work in the macrocosm so that supercomputers appear on our desks, networks in our homes and entertainment broadcasts in our hands.
- The transformation of operating and interface software into personal interactive digital pre-emptive agents.
- The transformation of poor performance into excellent performance through performance-enhancing drugs and embedded technology.
- The transformation of personal experiences – knowledge, dreams and fantasies – into mass experiences, first through advanced interactive cinematic technology and then through combinations of information, entertainment, education and communication technologies that use retina projection, leisure drugs and hypno-therapeutic technology.

Unless the strategist transforms his knowledge base and understanding he has no hope of transforming anything else and making a relevant impact on the world.

BEING INSIGHTFUL

The Master Strategist recognises patterns in the flow of information and sees new patterns from these patterns. We explored a number of the macro-level patterns of this type at the beginning of this chapter. However, this capability is one that is required to address the micro-level issues of life, as well as the most important macro-level issues.

As discussed earlier, things appear to run to a pattern that we recognise as 'normal'. We wish to believe that this is so as it allows us to subdue the fear that things may be out of (our) control. However, things are not as they seem, as it is only the 'surface' that moves to a 'normal' pattern.

The objective is to train strategists in pattern recognition, not just in analysis. This enables the Master Strategist to move beyond the linear, beyond the equation and beyond the machine, so he sees the pieces and forms a pattern.

BEING FORESIGHTFUL

The Master Strategist moves from pattern recognition to seeing new pattern possibilities and potential outcomes.

Strategy is two-fold: adaptation to survive and invention to gain. If we do not change in response to external changes we become irrelevant and so we die. The strategist must be able to see the changes required for survival. However, he must also be able to see the possibilities for creating new value. Strategists exploit the moving river to reach their destinations and, from the pieces of the puzzle, create their own pattern, thereby creating outcomes. Fundamentally, the strategist does not believe that there is only one possibility. There are many potential futures and each one can be created.

The Master Strategist sees not only the possible disruptions that could be triggered, but the triggers that could lead to new outcomes and the nature of the outcomes themselves.

The Master Strategist understands that the existing 'reality' is made up of pieces that can be re-cast and that this reality is always moving. He also sees the flow of this movement. Foresight comes from seeing the possibilities and the forks in the road. This is not about prediction, but about possibility.

BEING A RESULTS DELIVERER

When the stage of mature strategy has been reached, how will we know we are there? There are two clear indications. The first is internal to the strategist, and the second is in the quality of the outcomes of the strategist's advice.

On the first indication, ancient research took the form of meditation. The process of meditation involved cutting out the external environment, stilling the mind and letting the awareness go inwards. This inward journey was said to reveal the nature of one's body, emotions, mind and the objects of the mind. It would take one to a broader awareness of the interconnectedness and impermanence of all things. In the 20th and early 21st centuries, scientists have sought to establish the link between the brain's states (as evidenced by the brain waves emitted in these states) and physical, emotional and mental performance. The early research, carried out by institutes in the US such as Harvard University, has begun to establish the evidence that advanced meditative techniques do indeed lead to profound human mind-body capacities. Dr Herbert Benson of the Harvard Medical School points to changes in oxygen consumption, energy consumption and metabolism. Also finds meditators exhibits the low arterial lactate which is associated with the state of peace and tranquillity. In other words, meditation puts people into 'happy' and 'peaceful' states and into higher performance zones. Further research is likely to prove and re-establish the value of the meditation techniques developed by the Hindus and Buddhists thousands of years ago.

One of the key insights of the Master Strategist is that he is potentially an agent of change (a result) rather than a change agent (a cause). There is a dilemma at the heart of strategy: strategies are highly personal, in that their objective can be anything you want, but they are also highly impersonal, in that they must fit the situation and the environment. In the latter case, therefore, the objective of the strategy is nothing to do with you, it is a matter of fitness for purpose. Strategies are either effective or not in creating an intelligent adaptive system that achieves its purpose. The question that this dilemma points to is whether the purpose is yours or is one that does not belong to you. Are you, as the strategist, the inventor of the outcome or the agent of the outcome? Are your talents yours, so that you can do what you wish or are you bound to do only that which you are fit to do, in other words play your role? You have choice, but if you made inappropriate choices would you still be the Master Strategist?

The nature of the Master Strategist is that he naturally rises above the conflicting bodies and identifies a higher common position; he determines how to take whole, thereby minimises waste and destruction; and he sees an event as belonging within a flow of events, and so reacts within the context of the flow, not just to the event.

On the second indication, results, there is qualitative and quantitative evidence of the change. The more qualitative evidence will be in the nature of the strategies that are created by the Master Strategist. The strategies will have more of the character of revelation than analysis, will be more obtuse than trend projection, more dream-like than extended reality and more holistic than limited. On the more quantitative evidence, the strategies will be successful in delivering results, and will have certain characteristics. They will be:

> *Powerful* The Master Strategist will certainly be able to battle for superior power, but will be able to develop the most powerful strategies, which will enable him to win without having to fight.
>
> *Purposeful* The Master Strategist will be able to battle for superior purpose but will develop strategies that are inclusive and aspirational.
>
> *Principled* The Master Strategist will be able to battle for superior principles but others will wish to follow this strategy because of its superior principles and because of its lack of righteousness.

Such strategies will be directed at the underlying interconnected system rather than just the symptoms. They will address the fundamental essence of a situation with simplicity, clarity and honesty. The strategist will approach the situation with no fear of loss or greed for gain.

New Way: Beyond Strategy

Strategies become redundant when they have achieved their aim. To move beyond strategy itself we would need one of two circumstances to be present. The first is that the individual is beyond fear and greed. The second is that society is beyond fear and greed. The first is possible for each of us individually, while the second is unlikely in the world we live in but becomes possible when enough individuals have passed the first requirement.

The role of strategy is to move strategy closer to the realm where the fears and greeds are addressed not abused. Leaders in this realm would transform the negative energy into endeavours that promote peace, prosperity and freedom. The right-minded Master Strategists will have an impact in a way that touches a large mass of individuals and thereby creates the circumstances that foster a rise in human consciousness.

Ultimately, the Master Strategist cannot produce strategies for every eventuality. Therefore, the notion of strategy needs to be superseded by the notion of a strategic state. As we have explored in this work, the critical realisation is that, given the enormous number of potential moving elements in the world at any given time, it is not possible to continually create strategies to respond.

Our aim should be to place ourselves, our families, our communities, our institutions, our nations and our world in a strategic state that is powerful, principled and purposeful. This new state will provide us with a more sustainable system of life.

The challenge is no less than to create a new civilisation.

In the final chapter, we will draw together the outline of the case and reiterate some of the most important elements of the agenda for creating this new way.

7

THE AGENDA FOR THE FUTURE

There is no fixed agenda. There can be no fixed agenda, for it would not grow and, so, it would become irrelevant, and die.

Modern-day breakthroughs in science and technology have laid the foundation for other breakthroughs. Our ability to do the basic things that people do in life – work, entertain, communicate, cure themselves, kill enemies – has also seen dramatic breakthroughs. This explosion of breakthroughs has resulted in an explosion in information, which is suffocating our ability to make sense of what is happening. So, of course, we seek answers.

When Man needs answers, the answer-givers come.

Today's answer-givers have led us to believe in simple answers that play to our need for simplicity. Because of the sophistication of today's media and technology they are more effective than ever before at permeating our subconscious. Herein lies the real danger: in a world of ever-increasing change, we are willing to be satisfied with simplistic answers. This is a problem for each of us as citizens of the world.

We mechanistically follow rules and norms that prevent us from being shaken to the core. This is a self-defence survival pattern. However, it is also a suicide pattern. Events are moving faster than we are moving and we are becoming less and less fit to deal with them. We are not beyond the laws of nature. That which does not change becomes irrelevant and, over time, dies.

We stand on the brink of the greatest revolutions of science and consciousness. An era of miracles is upon us, which will enable us to alter the nature of our existence and our very being.

As has so often happened in history, the fruits of this may well be better weapons to wage faster and more effective wars. It certainly is not yet the means to wage faster and more effective peace. We need to create greater strategies to match our greater capability for good or ill.

Dangerous patterns of conflict are already in motion to test us. Great conflicts are appearing on the horizon and in our midst. The conflict players are set to play out these conflicts and the conflict-resolvers are unready. The time for conflict-resolvers is now. These will be the Master Strategists. They will be required to intervene to change the pattern of conflict, create new understanding and awareness and build new institutions to inculcate this awareness in others and allow it to grow.

It is in Man's nature to dream and aspire and then to endeavour, deceive and fight to achieve his dreams and aspirations. Strategy is merely the word we give to the thought that goes into determining how we will prevail. However, strategies can be formulated that maximise the chance of delivering 'good'. New principles are required to change our path onto this 'good' path. This is the role of great leaders, Master Strategists.

These results will not come without great effort on the part of the individual or without the right environment. This is the responsibility of the individual and of leaders.

There is a pressing need to question. There is a pressing

need also for honesty and courage. We must set a new agenda that addresses the most important questions:

- How many more wars must there be before we learn to establish peace?
- How many more feudal systems of enterprise before we learn to build prosperity?
- How many more inequitable regimes before we learn to honour freedoms and devote our greatest energies to finding the answers?

In this age of global access to people, places and the means to pay, there is nowhere to hide. We must find and deal better with those that fear and hate us or bear the consequences.

We will need to embrace a new language. This new language must come to change our minds. If we are successful, we will redefine power to mean the enhancement of freedoms; purpose will come to mean the pursuit of peace, prosperity and freedom; and principle will mean the pursuit of truth.

The resulting strategies will be more intuitive, more obtuse, more aspirational, more holistic, more technology-fused and, therefore, more uncomfortable.

Our success as humankind will only come if we put in place the institutions that will begin the work of demolishing the irrelevant, building the new and demolishing it once more when it becomes irrelevant.

We, therefore, stand at the door of an opportunity to seize the greatest personal power. We also stand at the door of the greatest opportunity in history – to create an Age of Peace, Prosperity and Freedom.

Preface

1 Throughout the book, $ denotes US dollars

2 'OECD Science, Technology and Industry Scoreboard 2003 – Towards a knowledge-based economy', OECD.

3 Hunger: the FAO estimates 815 million people undernourished in 1997 to 1999; 'Progress in providing safe water and sanitation for all during the 1990s: Report of the Secretary-General', United Nations, Economic and Social Council, Commission on Sustainable Development, 8th Session; World Health Report 1997, World Health Organisation; computer and internet penetration: International Telecommunications Union statistics for 2001: Computer penetration and Internet penetration covering E. Asia and Pacific, Latin America and Caribbean, Middle East and North Africa, South Asia and Sub-Saharan Africa compared to North America; genocide: www.hawaii.edn.

Chapter 1

1 Running Times, 2004 at runningtimes.com, Marathonguide.com for chart of times, *Guinness Book of World Records*, 2004.

2 UN Office on Drugs and Crime, Global Illicit Drug Trends, 2003; World Health Organisation, WHO European Health Communication Network, January 2002; 'Overweight and Obesity', British Nutrition Foundation, 2004.

3 Various timelines provide further details, including the *Encyclopaedia Britannica*, The History Channel and hyperhistory online.

4 IBM company site; *The Age of Intelligent Machines*,

Raymond Kurzweil, the MIT Press, 1990; Raj Reddy of Carnegie Mellon University.

5 'The Economic History of the Twentieth Century, Slouching Towards Utopia', draft outline paper, J. Brad DeLong, University of California at Berkeley.

6 'Music Piracy Report 2002'; Mitch Bainwol, Chairman, Recording Industry Association of America, at US Senate Hearing, September 2003; Pew Internet & American Life Project 2004, Harris Interactive, October 2004.

7 Falmouth Packet Archives regarding the steam ship *Sirius*; IATA Passenger Forecast 2000–2004, 2003–2007 and ICAO; WTM Global Travel Report, 2003.

8 *Four Thousand Years of Urban Growth: An Historical Census*, Tertius Chandler, the Edwin Mellen Press Ltd, 1989.

9 Population Reference Bureau 2004, World Urbanization Prospects, The 1999 Revision.

10 On China's silicon valleys and technology initiatives see multiple articles, 2002–2004, *The People's Daily*.

11 NASSCOM; Average Salary of Programmers, *CIO Magazine*, November 2002; Smart Access Survey, Merrill Lynch.

12 'The Economic History of the Twentieth Century, Slouching Towards Utopia', draft outline paper, J. Brad DeLong, University of California at Berkeley.

13 Throughout this work financial data such as market capitalisation statistics taken from Datastream and *Thomson Financial*.

14 For further information on the Asian crisis see the widely reported public sources, including 'A Three-Step Remedy for Asia's Financial Flu', R. Litan, February 1998, Brookings Institution; J. P. Morgan, World Financial Markets, First Quarter Report, 1998.

15 *Imperial Ends: The Decay, Collapse, and Revival of Empires*, Alexander J. Motyl, Columbia University Press, New York, 2001.

16 Widely reported approval by House of Representatives regarding Approval of Defense Budget, including BBC, *Wall Street Journal*, 7 November 2003; public sources.

17 WaterAid, 2004; United Nations Commission on Sustainable Development.

18 Transaction data taken from *Thomson Financial*.

Chapter 2

1 Quantum mechanics and uncertainty principle: original sources are 'Quantum Mechanics' and 'Uncertainty Principle', papers by Heisenberg, 1925 and 1927, respectively. Decent summaries are available from numerous published encyclopaedic sources. The Stanford University online library provides a good introduction.

Chaos theory: for an explanation of key principles and history of chaos theory-related thought see *Chaos: Making a New Science*, James Gleick, Vintage Minerva, 1996.

Synchronicity: for the origins see *On the Nature of the Psyche*, C. G. Jung, translated by R. F. C. Hull, Princeton University Press, 1969, and Wolfgang Pauli's paper on Synchronicity and the Collective Unconscious; *Synchronicity: The Bridge Between Matter and Mind*, David F. Peat, Bantam, June 1987, is an excellent exposition of the theory of and evidence for synchronicity.

2 Genius and creativity: *Scientific Genius: A Psychology of Science*, Dean Keith Simonton, Cambridge University Press, 1989 and *Greatness: Who Makes History and Why*, Dean Keith Simonton, Guildford Press, 1994. Dr Simonton studied 2,036 scientists throughout history to

form his conclusions.

3   J. P. Garnier, Chief Executive of the pharmaceutical giant GlaxoSmithKline, has in public interviews described the 'productivity crisis' in pharmaceutical research and development, see 'Turning the Tide of Pharmaceutical Productivity', *Scientific Computing*, 2004. Also see 'Innovation or Stagnation? Challenge and Opportunity on the Critical Path to New Medical Products', US Department of Health and Human Sciences, Food and Drug Administration, March 2004.

4   *Death By Government: Genocide and Mass Murder Since 1900*, Transaction Publishers (NJ), R. J. Rummel, 1994 (among other achievements, Finalist for 1996 Nobel Peace Prize). Also see www.hawaii.edn.

5   There are many good sources for environmental destruction. One of the simplest sources is The Ozone Hole Inc, a non-profit organisation dedicated to stopping the destruction of the ozone layer, preventing global warming and preserving the Earth's environment. For opinion linking political commitments, the environ-ment and human inequality, see Jeffrey Sachs, *The Economist*, 24 October 2002. Jeffrey Sachs is the director of the Earth Institute at Columbia University in New York.

Chapter 3

1   The phrase 'stream of consciousness' was coined in the West by William James (1842–1910) in 1890. James worked with Charles Sanders Peirce (1839–1914), an American mathematician, philosopher and logician. Both worked in the fields of psychology and philosophy to establish the philosophical school of thinking called pragmatism. Stream of consciousness was described by James as the set of constantly changing inner thoughts

and sensations which an individual has while conscious. Stream of consciousness is also a narrative technique in which a writer presents directly the uninterrupted flow of a character's thoughts, impressions and feelings, without the conventional devices of dialogue and description.

The Buddha expounded the doctrines of Transiency (*Anicca*), Sorrow (*Dukkha*) and No-Soul (*Anatta*) approximately 2,500 years ago. The Buddha explained that evil and good forces are latent in all Mankind. These evil forces rise to the surface at unexpected moments in varying strength. Enlightenment eradicates these forces and, as a result, one's stream of consciousness becomes perfectly purified.

Chapter 4

1 Chaos theory: for an explanation of key principles and history of chaos theory-related thought see *Chaos: Making a New Science*, James Gleick, Vintage Minerva, 1996.

2 See *Science, Order and Creativity*, David Bohm and David F. Peat, Taylor & Francis Ltd, 2000. Also *Infinite Potential: The Life and Times of David Bohm*, David F. Peat, Perseus Publishing, 1999.

3 IBM market share calculated as a percentage of market capitalisation of technology companies in hardware, software and services using Datastream.

4 Land mass analysis for Roman and British Empires taken from *Imperial Ends: The Decay, Collapse, and Revival of Empires*, Alexander J. Motyl, Columbia University Press, New York, 2001.

5 Microsoft's Windows Operating System is installed on 94 per cent of all personal computers sold in the world according to Forrester Research, 2004.

6 *Death by Government: Genocide and Mass Murder Since*

1900, Transaction Publishers (NJ) R. J. Rummel (among other achievements, Finalist for 1996 Nobel Peace Prize).

7   See *Self-Limiting Conflict: The Gandhian Style*, Paul Wehr, Westview Press, Boulder, Colorado, 1979.

8   OECD statistics on healthcare; *CIA World Factbook*, December 2003, for internet statistics; for military statistics see *CIA World Factbook*, December 2003, IISS (International Institute for Strategic Studies), 2001, *The Military Balance* 2001–2002, Taylor & Francis Ltd. Oxford: Oxford University Press, *Forbes 2004* on billionaires; on national pride see World Values Survey 2004.

9   There are numerous sources on GE and its transformation by Jack Welch. A good source of reference is the company itself on ge.com, from 2000 to December 2004 for data on GE and its initiatives, the number of businesses of GE as at 28 December 2004; market capitalisation from Datastream as at 28 December 2004.

10 Japanese resident cost vs. household income from *The Economist*; population statistics from 'Megacities and their Population', Population counter 1996; wage statistics as recorded in the 1998 edition of *Japan: An International Comparison*, a publication of the Japan Institute for Social and Economic Affairs.

11 Warren Buffet: there are numerous sources of which the Berkshire Hathaway site, in particular the annual reports, are a good source from the founder and executives. Warren Buffet's wealth taken from ranking according to *Forbes 2004*.

12 Information on SAR-11 bacterium from Indiana University Online Library, 2004.

Chapter 5

1   Kepler: there are multiple interesting sources, including *Johannes Kepler and the Music of the Spheres*, by David Plant at www.panplanet.com and horoscope produced by Kepler, discovered in December 1998 by Anthony Misch; on Isaac Newton see biographies such as *Isaac Newton*, James Gleick, Fourth Estate, 2003, and online sources as bbc.co.uk, Gottfried Leibniz: see *Leibniz, Mysticism and Religion*, Allison P. Coudert, Kluwer Academic Publishers, 1998; Matteo Ricci: see *The Memory Palace of Matteo Ricci*, Jonathan D. Spence, Penguin, 1985.

2   *How many people can the Earth support?*, David Pimentel, Population Press, March/April 1999 (Vol. 5, No. 3), The Population Coalition.

3   Compiled by Dr McCluney, Principal Research Scientist with the Florida Solar Energy Center in Cocoa, FL, a Research Institute of the University of Central Florida in Orlando; Reference to survival based on numbers from Paul Jindra.